There's no greater investment you can make with your time, talent, and treasure than to give to the Great Commission. I've been standing shoulder to shoulder with Erick as he pushes forward to bring the love of Jesus to every nation, tribe, and tongue. This book will help you activate your God-given gifts in the greatest adventure this side of eternity.

Bruce Wilkinson
New York Times best-selling author and speaker

Erick's influence has been a crucial foundation underneath everything I have done in my life and ministry. I know his remarkable message will inspire and equip you, as well. We may not be called to a full-time foreign ministry, but we are ALL called to a full-time life of sharing the Good News wherever we are.

Shaunti Feldhahn
Best-selling author of *For Women Only and For Men Only*

I have been personally challenged by Erick's commitment to ask the question "'What would serve Jesus best?'" in every phase of his life. Erick's life and the stories in his book serve as an invitation to all of us to ask and answer that question in our own lives.

Dr. Steve Douglass
President, Campus Crusade for Christ/Cru

Everyone, Everywhere

Everyone, Everywhere

Glimpses of God's Global Work
Through People Like You

DR. ERICK SCHENKEL

We love hearing from our readers. Please contact us at www.anekopress.com/questions-comments with any questions, comments, or suggestions.

Visit the Jesus Film Project website: www.jesusfilm.org

Everyone, Everywhere – Dr. Erick Schenkel

Copyright © 2016

First edition published 2017

Printed in the United States of America

Aneko Press – *Our Readers Matter*™

www.anekopress.com

Aneko Press, Life Sentence Publishing, and our logos are trademarks of Life Sentence Publishing, Inc.

203 E. Birch Street

P.O. Box 652

Abbotsford, WI 54405

RELIGION / Christian Ministry / Evangelism

Paperback ISBN: 978-1-62245-482-2

eBook ISBN: 978-1-62245-483-9

10   9   8   7   6   5   4   3

Available where books are sold

Contents

Preface

This book is an invitation to everyone to join the most compelling, the most compassionate, the most significant movement in the world. It is an account of the remarkable works of God through people. God is showing His love to millions of people around the world through heroes and martyrs, through students and villagers, through simple, personal expressions of His love by millions of His followers.

Many of the stories told here involve the *JESUS* film and other films created by the Jesus Film Project, the organization I have the privilege of serving as executive director. In fact, a desire to pass along some of the wonderful stories we receive weekly is one of my reasons for writing this book. My special thanks to my fellow staff members and those of partner organizations who have faithfully recorded and passed along these stories.

But my deeper reason for writing is to call renewed attention to the Great Commission of Jesus Christ, to His heart to restore everyone, everywhere to a personal, eternal relationship with Himself. The Jesus Film Project is grateful to be part of a global movement of followers of Jesus that is known in the USA as Cru, with whom we share a passion for connecting people with God's love. There is no more important work on earth, and none more challenging or exciting, as you will see in the pages ahead. Thanks are due to many colleagues who helped with the preparation of this book, and especially to Josh Newell and his team for bringing it to publication.

I am deeply grateful to my wife, Elizabeth, with whom I have had the privilege of experiencing this great adventure, and to our children for their love and inspiration throughout our journey.

As a leader in a Great Commission movement, I always try to ask the question, "What serves Jesus best?" instead of "What serves me best?" or "What serves my organization best?" I hope this book will serve to challenge you to become ever more deeply involved in serving Jesus in the mission that He committed to all who follow Him. Let's do this together. Let us take the message of His love to everyone, everywhere, and invite them to enjoy with us a real and eternal relationship with God.

Chapter 1

Living the Great Adventure

As I knelt over the badly broken body of my wife, Elizabeth, on the floor of our mud-walled Central Asian home, a long line of those who had suffered for following our Master flashed through my mind. I said to her though my own bloodied lips, "Don't worry honey, someday you'll look back on this as the best day of your life." At that moment, I honestly didn't know if she would live or die. But I knew that, either way, my words to her would be true.

We had moved to our Central Asian home from a typical American suburb four years earlier, taking along four of our children and leaving our fifth at college. In many ways it hadn't been a good time to move, but as we assessed our lives, we realized that there would never be a good time to do what we were sensing God's call to do. We left a comfortable home, sold two cars, gave away our family dog and cat, left town sports and dance lessons and everything we knew, to move to a country whose name we hadn't even known a little over a year before.

We had been living the American dream. I'd been plucked from my poor public school in northern Kentucky to attend Harvard College. I had recently received my fourth diploma from Harvard – a PhD in the study of world religions. I was leading a small evangelical congregation and teaching part-time at a prestigious local university. I'd recently taken a third job at an evangelical New England preparatory school that enabled me to continue to preach weekly and actually make ends meet financially – a real dream for a pastor. And yet, something deeply troubled me.

Many people had warned me that it was not a good idea for an evangelical Christian to study the world's religions and cultures at a place like Harvard; they were afraid I might lose my faith. In fact, my studies led me to a conclusion that was even more troubling. My faith was fine; it was my lifestyle that was a problem!

I professed to know God personally through Jesus Christ and to believe that God loved everyone and wanted every person on earth to know Him as I did. Yet my lifestyle remained unaffected by the reality that over vast portions of the earth, it remained extremely unlikely that some people whom God deeply loved would ever have a chance to hear the message of God's love in Jesus Christ.

I became familiar with something called the "10/40 window," the rectangular area of North Africa, the Middle East, and Asia between 10 and 40 degrees north latitude, home to nearly five billion people – 60% of the world's population.

This region is home to Islam, Buddhism, Hinduism, Sikhism, and Shintoism; over one-fourth of its people have never even heard the message of Jesus Christ.

I learned that when it comes to funding the work of sharing the good news about Jesus, 87% of the money goes for work among those already Christian, 12% for work among those already evangelized but non-Christian, and 1% for work among unevangelized and unreached people. Only 0.1% of all Christian giving is directed toward missionary efforts in the thirty-eight least evangelized countries in the world, most of which are in the 10/40 window.[1]

I began to look for resources to share what I was discovering about the world with my high school students. I found the *JESUS* film, a feature film taken from the Gospel of Luke that was being widely translated and used for pioneer evangelism in unreached areas. I read a book by Jesus Film Project founder Paul Eshleman, called *I Just Saw* JESUS, which documented the miracles that were taking place and churches that were being planted as a result of film showings.[2]

I thought of my new job in this prestigious school. A hundred and twenty-six people had applied for the job, and I had gotten it! Good for me! Then I heard the question in my mind: "Do you really think that none of those other hundred and twenty-five people could have done this job?" I thought about the work of church planting I was reading about, how significant it was in God's mind, and how few people were answering the call to the unevangelized. The question came to mind, "Why don't you let someone else take this job and you go do the other one?" As I wrestled with the idea, the thought came to me, which has become a deep conviction over the years since: "The best jobs in the world are the ones nobody wants!"

At about this time, I took a week off from my responsibilities as pastor and teacher to attend a large conference for New England Christian leaders. I was glad to have a break from my tiring routine and was desperately hoping to be refreshed. I hid myself away in the back row where I could ponder things in the loneliness of the crowd, and I was somewhere between praying and dozing as Richard Foster talked about his new book, *Prayer.* Then he told this story:

The best jobs in the world are the ones nobody wants!

> A disciple once came to Abba Joseph, saying, "Father, according as I am able, I keep my little rule, my little fast, and my little prayer. And according as I am able, I strive to cleanse my mind of all evil thoughts and my heart of all evil intents. Now, what more should I do?" Abba Joseph rose up and stretched out his hands to heaven, and his fingers became like ten lamps of flame. He answered, "Why not be totally changed into fire?"[3]

I don't know why God chose to use the words of Abba Joseph to stir my heart; there was nothing in my background that would make a desert monk my go-to source of inspiration. But when I heard those words, something was released inside me. I suddenly didn't care about what job I held or what I accomplished. All I wanted to do was to be close to Jesus, to be on fire with love from Him, for Him, and for others because of Him – to live my whole life on fire with Him. Nothing else mattered. I lived in the glow of those words for months, and I can honestly say, more than twenty years later, they influence me still.

As Elizabeth and I continued to process what we were learning about the need of the world for Jesus, we realized that we were not particularly well suited for rural villages like those where much of the *JESUS* film work was taking place. But the Muslim world came to mind. I had studied quite a bit of Islamic history and philosophy in my doctoral program and had grown to appreciate the rich intellectual heritage of this tradition. Despite their awareness of Jesus, called "Isa" in the Qur'an, most Muslims had never heard the actual message of Jesus as told in the Gospels. We began to sense God's call to share about Jesus Christ with Muslims, and we even looked for a chance to travel in a Muslim country.

Then one Sunday a young woman stood up in our church congregation and made an announcement that her local student ministry had adopted a former-Soviet Muslim city as a partner and was planning to send a team there. We supported this venture, and a year later we were setting our affairs in order and moving to the other side of the world, to this wonderful, mysterious, unpredictable place with the mud-walled houses, to work in education and economic development and to plant churches alongside *JESUS* film teams and university student movements.

After four years, we were beginning to find our stride. I had become accustomed to long hours, working as a university teacher and devoting as much time as possible to the growing underground Christian movement in this Islamic republic. Elizabeth and I had been working with a student church in the capital city and with *JESUS* film teams across the country. We'd established a thriving Bible school in the regional language, and we were ready to begin instruction in the traditional national language.

Then, the morning we were to begin instruction in the national language, Elizabeth awakened me at 4:00 a.m. with a shout, "Honey, wake up. They're here!" As I dreamily pondered who "they" were, a man dressed in a black running suit and gloves, his face covered in a black ski mask, began to beat me with a wooden-handled metal hatchet. I looked across the bed and another man, dressed the same way, was beating Elizabeth with a similar weapon.

My first thought was, "OK, Lord, it's been great; see you in a minute." We had heard of the Muslim extremists called "wahhabists," who attacked with hatchets, knocked their victims unconscious, and then beheaded them. (We now know they were our adopted country's al-Qaeda affiliate.) I called on the name of Jesus, remembering stories of people who had been delivered from various situations by calling on His name.

After receiving several blows, I realized my assailant was hitting me with the blunt side of the hatchet – not the sharp blade. The thought came that he was trying to give me a good beating (and this certainly qualified as a good beating) but not kill me. Maybe it was not my time to die. I began to resist and offer the attackers money, hoping that maybe they could be bought. As I wrestled my attacker across the room to get the money, I realized that the man beating Elizabeth had already finished his work. She was lying on the floor in a pool of blood. As I shoved a few dollars at the man, he seemed to allow me to wrest the hatchet from his hand and the two of them fled.

I assessed my own wounds – some broken teeth, a broken finger, numerous bruises, and rapidly swelling lumps all over my head. But Elizabeth had fared far worse. The first blow she'd taken had fractured her skull. A subsequent one had shattered her right arm, leaving her defenseless, and she suffered two additional skull fractures. But she was alive! I ran out to look for our two daughters, aged 8 and 12, and the young American woman who was living with us and helping us with our work. I did not know if they had been taken, killed, or had escaped.

My daughters had been asleep in their room when the first of the attackers opened their door, flicked on a cigarette lighter, peered in, and quickly moved on. My older daughter saw a light coming through the window and felt she should take her sister and go out the window. This enabled the two of them to avoid the three men in the house, but not a fourth man standing guard at our gate. He raised a hatchet over my youngest, and then his hand began to shake. He said, "You don't understand what's happening here; run away!" I found them hiding in a chicken coop at the back of our yard, unhurt but badly shaken.

Our young associate had tried to call the police when she heard us being beaten but was struck in the head with a hatchet before managing to flee the house and climb the fence into the neighbor's yard. I found her using all the local language she knew to explain to our neighbors what had happened.

After locating my daughters and our colleague, I left them with our neighbors and returned to Elizabeth. She was in and out of consciousness, temporarily partially blinded and in great pain. I did not know if she would live or die, and I prayed for

"Honey, someday you will look back on this as the best day of your life."

something I could say to comfort her. I heard myself say, "Honey, someday you will look back on this as the best day of your life."

Her first thought was, "Not anytime soon!" Then she thought of Jim Elliot, David Brainerd, and countless others who had lost their lives in service to those who had never heard the good news, and the contribution their lives had made. In the midst of her pain, she found comfort.

My words turned out to be true in so many ways. That was the best day of Elizabeth's life, and mine. We were evacuated by emergency services and treated in Europe and then in the USA, but we each returned as quickly as we were able. When the precious people of that country saw us come back, they saw God's love for them through us in a clearer way than we could have ever imagined possible. We were able to make a lasting contribution to many lives in that region over the next twelve years, partly as a result of that day.

This is a book about reaching everyone, everywhere with the good news of Jesus Christ. That is not merely an intellectual proposition for me and mine, though I have thought a lot about it, and invite you here to think about it with me. It is a commission – a job we've been given to accomplish. One that requires action. Jesus has asked us to take His love to everyone in the world. Think it over. And then do something. You will find the best days of your life.

Chapter 2

The Book's One Story

I first heard the phrase "Great Commission" while I was sitting on the floor of a large meeting room in a residence house at Harvard College as an overmatched first year student from Kentucky, accepted to the college on its regional diversity policy. A few months earlier, I had heard the Christian gospel clearly presented for the first time by one of my high school teachers, and I had made a decision to become a disciple of Jesus Christ, although I understood very little of what that might mean. Now I was sitting in a meeting of the Christian Fellowship with several dozen other students as the speaker made his case from the Bible.

Great Commission? I joked to myself, "I guess a great commission would be about 30 percent of the profit on the sale."

The speaker continued, "If I had the privilege of writing a news story about the greatest events of all the centuries, one of the most important would be a meeting on a mountain near Galilee, where a small group of men were given a global strategy for carrying God's love and forgiveness to a lost and dying world. On this mountain, these men received the greatest challenge ever given to mankind, by the greatest person who ever lived, concerning the greatest power ever revealed and the greatest promise ever recorded.

"I refer, of course, to the Great Commission of our Lord Jesus Christ, which He gave to His disciples, and through them, to us. He said, 'Go into all the world and make disciples of all nations, baptizing them in the name of the Father, the Son, and the Holy Spirit, teaching them to observe all that I have commanded. And, lo I am with you always, even to the end of the age.' Jesus Christ gave this command, the Great Commission to all of His followers. It is up to each one of us to do everything we can to fulfill it."[4]

I was still trying to get my bearings as a follower of Jesus, and now I was being told that Jesus had a serious plan for my life!

The speaker continued by quoting Dr. Bill Bright,

Most Christians have never taken this command of our Lord seriously. We have been playing games while our world is in flames. We are like men and women who are straightening pictures on the walls of a burning building. We are dealing with peripheral issues when it is the hearts of people that need to be changed. The problems in the world that are threatening

> to engulf humanity can only be solved
> through faith in Christ and obedience to
> His commands.
>
> If we take our Lord seriously, we must
> dedicate ourselves fully – time, talent, and
> treasure – to the fulfillment of the Great
> Commission, not out of a sense of legalistic
> duty, but out of love and gratitude for what
> Christ has done for us.[5]

I cannot say that I understood all the speaker was trying to say that night, but I knew I had come face-to-face with the most exciting challenge ever presented in all of human history, issued by the most important person who ever lived.

My wife tells me I am a redneck with a thin Harvard veneer; she's probably right. But my values have not been formed primarily by my Kentucky upbringing or my Ivy League education, but by a commitment to serious examination of and obedience to the Book, the Bible, the Word of God.

The more I have read and studied the Book, the more convinced I have become of the central importance of the Great Commission to every person, everywhere in the world.

You see, the whole Bible tells one single story. Scholars call it the meta-narrative of the Bible. It goes something like this:

God created humans to live in paradise in life-giving relationship with Himself. But the humans turned away from him by doing the one thing He had asked them not to do, and this love relationship was broken. The result was continual human transgressions of all kinds – hatred, murder, injustice, and cruelty. And the punishment for this sin was death, the eternal torment of separation from God.

But God promised that He would one day restore that original fellowship. He chose one family and made a nation of them so that He could show the whole world through them the beauty of living in restored relationship to God. He also promised that One would be born in this nation who would be called "God with us" and who would offer a restored relationship with God to people from every nation.

Go into all the world and preach the Good News to everyone, everywhere.

That One was Jesus Christ. He lived a life like no other, a life that showed God's goodness and love. He preached deliverance to captives and proclaimed the restored justice of God. He was killed on a cross by political and religious leaders, but God raised Him from the dead, demonstrating that He was indeed sent from God.

After His resurrection, Jesus commanded His disciples to go to everyone in the world and offer all people the chance to be restored to God and become part of His eternal family through faith in Jesus' death on the cross for them.

All four of the gospels confirm this sending, this Great Commission of Jesus recorded in Matthew 28. In Mark 16:15, Jesus says, *Go into all the world and preach the Good News to everyone, everywhere* (Living Bible).

Luke reports in chapter 24: *Then he opened their minds so they could understand the Scriptures. He told them, "This is what is written: The Messiah will suffer and rise from the dead on the third day, and repentance for the forgiveness of sins will be preached in his name to all nations, beginning at Jerusalem."* In the first chapter of Acts, verse 8, Luke returns to this theme, quoting Jesus as saying, *You will receive power when the Holy Spirit comes on you, and you will be my witnesses in Jerusalem, and in all Judea and Samaria, and to the ends of the earth.* John puts it quite simply: *Again Jesus said, "Peace be with you! As the Father has sent me, I am sending you"* (John 20:21).

All these passages make clear the *command* of Jesus to go to everyone, everywhere, but I especially love the passages that make clear His *heart* – the reason God has sent Him and He has sent us. So many gospel stories reveal God's heart. One is the story of the calling of Matthew:

> *As Jesus went on from there, he saw a man named Matthew sitting at the tax collector's booth. "Follow me," he told him, and Matthew got up and followed him.*
>
> *While Jesus was having dinner at Matthew's house, many tax collectors and sinners came and ate with him and his disciples. When the Pharisees saw this, they asked his disciples, "Why does your teacher eat with tax collectors and sinners?"*
>
> *On hearing this, Jesus said, "It is not the*

healthy who need a doctor, but the sick.
But go and learn what this means: 'I
desire mercy, not sacrifice.' For I have not
come to call the righteous, but sinners."
(Matthew 9:9-13)

Jesus did not come for religious people; He came for those who know they need God! He came for the broken, for the hopeless, for all who humbly receive Him.

And He cares for every last person! In Luke 15, Jesus tells three stories: one about a lost sheep, one about a lost coin, and one about a lost son. The lesson of each story is the same: Heaven rejoices when one person is restored to God. There are parties in heaven for people who take God's offer of a "second chance." What an amazing God. He loves people so much He dies for them and then rejoices when one returns to Him!

Jesus will not return until the job He has given to His followers is done!

The Bible teaches that Jesus will return to the earth to establish a kingdom of justice and peace. But Jesus will not return until the job He has given to His followers is done.

In Matthew 24:14, Jesus says, *This gospel of the kingdom will be preached in the whole world as a testimony to all nations, and then the end will come.* The word translated "nations" is *ethnos*; it literally means ethnic groups or people groups. Until the good news has reached every people group, it cannot reach every person, because each person must be reached in terms of his own language and culture.

But Jesus' heart is not simply that the good news reach every people group. His heart is for every *person*. When writing about why Jesus had not yet returned, the apostle Peter said, *The Lord is not slow in keeping his promise, as some understand slowness. Instead he is patient with you, **not wanting anyone to perish, but everyone to come to repentance*** (2 Peter 3:9).

God is not willing that any perish! He wants *everyone* to come to repentance. One day Jesus will return to earth to set everything right – every injustice will be remedied, every wrong righted, and every tear wiped away. Yet today, because of His patience, He waits, because He wants every person to have a chance to come into a personal relationship with Him that will last for all eternity.

> *For God was in Christ, reconciling the world to himself, no longer counting people's sins against them. And he gave us this wonderful message of reconciliation.*
> (2 Corinthians 5:19 NLT)

Jesus' Great Commission to His people is to go to *every person* with the good news that God wants them to be reconciled to Himself. Yet today, only about two billion of the world's seven billion people have accepted this gift of being reconciled to God. God's heart is for the five billion who are yet to be reconciled to Him.

In Central Asia I had the privilege of being friends with Dr. Azim and Amira Gaziev from the ancient city of Bukhara. As the birthplace of Imam al-Bukhari (creator of the second most holy book in the Muslim religion) and the burial place of the region's most renowned Sufi, Bakhouddin Naqshbandi, Bukhara is considered by Muslims to be a holy city. Amira gloried in Bukhara's history and religion. Her profession was to paint the Qur'anic verses on public buildings and teach Arabic to the city's imams.

> **He has given us the wonderful job of announcing this good news to everyone.**

Azim had pursued a different course. As the son of the professor of Marxist philosophy at Bukhara State University, steeped in Soviet atheism, he chose to study medicine and become a doctor.

Then Amira discovered the Book. She was given a copy by a European woman who had come to work in the city. Much of its teaching was familiar to her: there is one God, God is creator, God is just, God will judge the world. But what a different story it told about what God is doing today. Yes, He will judge the world with justice, but that is not what He is doing now.

Jesus' death on the cross showed her that God is a God who would rather die for His enemies than kill them! And He has given us the wonderful job of announcing this good news to everyone.

The true followers of God are not on a jihad to punish evildoers, but on a mission to give them a chance to return to God. We have the opportunity to love a broken world where injustice and unkindness are real and at times horrible. Some religious zealots offer as a solution the establishment of God's law by human force, by holy war. The Bible tells us that there will indeed be a day when God will set all things right, but He will do it Himself and in His own time. He is not slow, as some people think, but He is patient with us, not wanting anyone to die, but wanting all to return to Him.

Our task in this life is not to try to make people obey God by force, but to announce to every person that God is patiently withholding judgment because He wants that person to have an intimate relationship with Him. I am shocked when I hear Christians speak of their enemies with hatred and respond to acts of terror perpetrated against Christians with a desire for vengeance. I am encouraged every time I hear a Christian friend from a Middle Eastern country pray for both the victims and the terrorists, because he understands that God loves them both.

God loves every person on earth and wants to have a personal relationship with each and every one. He does not love some nationalities more than others. He does not love some races more than others. He does not love the rich more than the poor. He loves the oppressed and the oppressor.

My Central Asian friend Amira became a follower of Jesus, the one who brought mercy to sinners. After initially rejecting Amira and her newfound revelation of God, her husband, Azim, also became a follower of Jesus. They now live their lives in obedience to the Great Commission, spreading the good news about God and Jesus wherever they go and with everyone they meet. They have seen hundreds become His followers, including many of their family members. They have been driven from their home country – and from a nearby country to which they fled – yet they continue in the mission of Jesus.

We live in a time when spiritual warfare in the world is becoming more intense. A tragically false idea of God's mission to the world is drawing deeply committed followers. The contrast is clear: the Great Commission or Global Jihad.

It is time for the followers of Jesus Christ to give their hearts and souls and minds and strength to serve in the true mission of God. This is a mission of love, of mercy, of forgiveness, of hope, of eternal life.

The real story of God is just too good not to be told!

God loved the world so much that He sent His only Son, that whoever believes in Him would not die, but would have eternal life (John 3:16). And His Son is sending His followers into the world to tell everyone, everywhere about this good news.

Let's go!

Chapter 3

Everything We Say and Do

"Preach the gospel at all times; when necessary use words." These words have been attributed to St. Francis of Assisi, although scholars have never been able to confirm that he actually said them.

The quote is often used to express the position that when it comes to communicating the good news of Jesus, good works are always more important than good words, that doing is always more important than preaching.

But this is not entirely true. With regard to the question, How should we show the love of God?

    a. By good works

    b. By preaching

The correct answer is always:

    Both "a" and "b."

History and Scripture affirm this.

Since Francis is often cited in this discussion, let's start with a closer look at what he actually did say and do. Francis's biographers have found that he clearly affirmed the absolute importance of both proclaiming and living the good news. In his day he was known as much for his preaching as for his lifestyle. He traveled from village to village, often visiting as many as five in a day, preaching to all who would listen – the rich and the poor, women and men, merchants and peasants. He'd preach atop hay bales or from the steps of a public building. His preaching was quite animated; he took the style of the troubadours of his day, bringing people to laughter and tears as he vividly portrayed the stories of the gospels. Contrary to the image of Francis as a mild mannered nature lover, his preaching could be both comforting and challenging. He called both great and small to repent of their sins and live a life in keeping with their repentance. He also instructed his followers to preach, sending them out two by two into the surrounding villages and beyond. In one of the most amazing episodes of the era, he actually crossed the battle lines during a crusade to preach the good news to the Caliph of Egypt!

At the same time, Francis's message left no room for a shallow or hypocritical response to the good news. He actually *did* say, "It is no use walking anywhere to preach unless our walking is our preaching." Not as catchy a phrase as the one usually attributed to him, but a more nuanced expression of the need for both preaching and lifestyle.[6]

So why has the thing that Francis did not say become so popular? I'll offer two reasons.

First, there will always be a human tendency to shrink from the opposition that the good news inevitably brings. Calling people back to God implies that they need to turn from things they are doing that displease God and from a self-determined way of life. This call will always make some people mad.

> We think that people will figure out the good news just by seeing our changed lives, but they don't.

Yet we know that on the other side of repentance is a beautiful life of love and service to others. Better, some might reason, just to show the results of a repentant life and not really have to deal with the possible negative response to the preaching.

The problem is, this doesn't work. We think that people will figure out the good news just by seeing our changed lives, but they don't.

I heard the story of a man who thought he was doing a good job living the good news before his non-Christian coworker, only to have him say, "Oh, I didn't know you were a Christian. I thought you were just a good person, and I thought it was OK not to become a Christian since you showed me an example of a good person who was not a Christian."

The second reason the pseudo-quote from Faux-Francis has become so popular is that many western Christians desperately want to address the fact that the modern revivalist style of church life, based only on preaching and profession, is sometimes tragically unbalanced. It has often emphasized only proclamation and belief without demanding lifestyle change from either the proclaimer or the hearer. This kind of intellectualized reduction of Christianity will never appeal to most people, and it will never please God.

Many scholars have traced the development of this tragic divide between proclamation and good works in modern Christianity. It has been called the "Great Reversal" and "The Hole in Our Gospel."[7] Theologians have blamed it on a misunderstanding of grace and a neglect of the importance of good works in the life of the follower of Jesus. Historians have pointed to the rise of social gospel liberalism that drove conservative evangelicals to emphasize *only* propositional faith in response to the liberal tendency to give attention *only* to good works. In turn, this has led some evangelicals to stress good works over evangelism.

We need to end this vicious cycle of imbalance!

The truth is, preaching and good works are designed to work together to proclaim the good news. In fact, good works are designed by God to be the apologetic for our words. James certainly says this: *Show me your faith without your works, and I will show you my faith by my works* (James 2:18 NKJV). We sometimes forget that Paul taught the same thing; his entire letter to Titus is about showing faith by good works: *Let our people learn to devote themselves to good works, so as to help cases of urgent need, and not be unfruitful* (Titus 3:14 ESV).

Paul may *seem* to have emphasized faith over works when dealing with the heresy that obedience to the law was necessary for salvation, but a careful reading of his letters shows that he often stressed the necessity of Christian lifestyle as the validation of the good news he preached.

Proclamation and good works together compellingly present the good news. The most effective missional groups in the church's history have always understood that.

In our day of specialization, this often means that interdepartmental and interagency cooperation are necessary to insure that both preaching and practical expressions of Christian love are present where the good news is being extended. Some of our most exciting Jesus Film Projects are partnerships with aid organizations like Global Aid Network (GAiN), Global Hope, World Relief, and other Christian humanitarian assistance agencies. Many of these partners are part of the Accord Network, which exists to help Christ-centered organizations achieve the best in relief and development.

> God loves people. When they hurt, He feels their pain.

God loves people. When they hurt, He feels their pain. He does not start caring for their welfare only when they die. He cares for their lives here and now. The message of the Kingdom of God that Jesus came preaching has present as well as future aspects. God's kingdom of justice and love has broken through into the present age, and His followers pray and work to see His will done on earth, as it is in heaven. The future will see the full establishment of His kingdom, when He returns to fully establish His reign. There is no contradiction between working for God's will to be done on earth and continuing to long for heaven.

Kingdom work is essential, but there is no kingdom without preaching, because we must be born again to see the kingdom. And it is through the foolishness of a preached message that God has chosen to save the lost (1 Corinthians 1:21).

Let us live as the real Saint Francis, preaching by word and by deed, to everyone, everywhere.

Chapter 4

Using Every Means

B ill Bright, founder of Campus Crusade for Christ, now called Cru in the USA, dreamed of making a film on the life of Jesus Christ, but he had a hard time getting much support for the idea. It was still in the early days of Hollywood, and the film industry was viewed by many as a distributor of only the worst kinds of stories. Many people had reservations about the impact of showing the face of a human actor as the face of the Son of God. Would it be idolatry or lead to idolatry? Finally, some brave pioneers took a chance on the idea, and the rest is history. The *JESUS* film has been used by God to bring the message of salvation through Jesus Christ to the world in more than seven billion viewings, in more than 1,500 languages.

Bill saw the potential of a technical innovation – film – to fulfill the Great Commission, because he was intent on reaching everyone. Our deepest life commitments will always determine the way we see the world.

Some people look at the latest information technologies and see great potential for harm, and certainly that potential is real. When we understand the heart of God to reach everyone with His love, and when we understand His involvement in every area of human life, we expect to find a way for every technological innovation to serve His grand purpose of making Himself known to everyone.

Those who are intent on enabling everyone to know Jesus look on the information technology revolution as the latest and greatest means of proclaiming His good news.

Let's look for just a moment at how God has used technology throughout the history of the church.

When Bible scholars reflect on the words of the apostle Paul in Galatians 4:4: *But when the fullness of time had come, God sent forth his Son* (ESV), many point to the cultural developments of the Greco-Roman world as one reason that God sent Jesus into the world when and where He did. The Roman Empire provided a common culture and language and a system of roads that enabled the apostles to reach much of the world with the good news relatively quickly.

God has used technology throughout the history of the church.

Perhaps the most important technological innovation for the spreading of the good news was the book. Before the printing press was invented – more than 1,400 years after Jesus gave His Great Commission – people did not have books. The "Bible" as we know it – a book that is available to most people and can be carried around and read at any time – simply did not exist. Jesus never had this kind of Bible; neither did Paul. Yet we can scarcely imagine how to develop a relationship with God without a Bible. The invention of the printing press and the mass production of books was not an unmixed blessing. Most of the books published in the last five-hundred-plus years have not had the purpose of glorifying God or spreading His message. Yet it is easy to see how the book, especially the Bible in book form, has been a tool used by God to get His message to everyone, everywhere.

The twentieth century opened with another breakthrough in communication technology: the invention of the radio. Guglielmo Marconi, its inventor, understood the potential of his creation for good and for evil. "Have I done the world good, or have I added a menace," he asked.[8] The answer was "Yes, and yes." The radio was another tool that, in itself, was neutral. It would be used for much good and for much evil. Marconi himself attempted to tip the scales in the good direction by offering his services free of charge to the Vatican, so that the church could use radio to evangelize the nations. Marconi introduced Pope Pius XI for the first broadcast of Vatican Radio, saying, "With the help of Almighty God, who allows the many mysterious forces of nature to be used by man, I have been able to prepare this instrument which will accord to the Faithful of all the world the consolation of hearing the voice of the Holy Father."[9]

American Protestants were especially quick to use radio as a tool to reach people for Christ. In the 1930s and 1940s, programs such as the *Back to God Hour* with Henry Schultze and Peter Eldersveld, the *Radio Bible Class* with M. R. DeHaan, and the *Old-Fashioned Revival Hour* with Charles Fuller were among America's most popular radio programs. In 1935, *The Lutheran Hour* with Walter Maier was reaching approximately 1,200 stations worldwide in thirty-six languages with an estimated audience of 700 million (a third of the world's population at that time). Although some feared that radio broadcast was not a worthy medium for the good news since it might lower religion to the level of mere entertainment, most saw in radio the possibility of making world evangelization a reality.[10]

Trans World Radio was founded in 1954 in Tangier, Morocco, to broadcast into fascist Spain. Today it is the largest evangelical media organization in the world, comprising more than seventy-five partners and broadcasting the good news in over 200 languages, including to the most difficult to reach areas of the world.[11]

In 1952, American Pentecostal evangelist Rex Humbard recalled, "I saw this new thing called television and I said, 'That's it. God has given us that thing . . . the most powerful force of communication, to take the gospel into . . . every state in the Union.'" Soon, Oral Roberts and Billy Graham were televising their crusades and pioneering the use of this "new thing" to reach not only America, but beyond.[12]

In 1961, Pat Robertson founded the Christian Broadcasting Network (CBN) in Portsmouth, Virginia, broadcasting from a UHF television station with a signal that barely reached across the city limits. Soon CBN's new talk show format, *The 700 Club,* would prove to be the ideal ministry match for this new medium. As of 2016, CBN programs have aired in 62 languages in 147 countries, and CBN has given birth to major humanitarian and educational efforts around the world.[13]

In 1973, Trinity Broadcasting Network was founded by Paul and Jan Crouch; it has become the largest Christian network, featured on over 5,000 television stations, over 70 satellites, the internet, and thousands of cable systems around the world.[14]

Dozens of other broadcasters have followed these pioneers, and today even the most difficult areas of the world have been extensively reached by Christians through television broadcasts. Christian television is no longer just a medium used by the Western church to reach into other cultures; Christian TV broadcast is a global phenomenon. For example, since 1966, Sat-7 has broadcast "Christian television by and for the people of the Middle East and North Africa" with over 80 percent of their content created in the region.[15]

The latest technological revolution to reshape communication is the internet. In the late 1980s, ARPANET, a military communications network, was released to the public. It has transformed the way we handle information of all kinds, and is remaking global relationships.

What do you associate with the internet? Distorted information, invasion of privacy, online pornography? Certainly those are real, but many of us see the internet as yet another tool for the fulfillment of the Great Commission.

One social commentator has said of the internet's

impact, "Take the word 'local.' It once referred to your own street, town, or even the state you lived in, but now *everywhere* is local…. Where once our reach was limited by physical boundaries, today almost everyone and everything is just a digital handshake away."[16] Think of the words of Jesus: *You will be my witnesses in Jerusalem, and in all Judea and Samaria, and to the ends of the earth* (Acts 1:8). The internet makes "the ends of the earth" a digital handshake away.

Recently, my friend Tom Cannavino was riding in a hotel shuttle bus and noticed that the driver had an accent. Tom asked and learned that his name was James, and he was from Kenya. When Tom asked what language he spoke, James told him, "Luo." Tom went to the Jesus Film Project app on his phone and selected "maps." He then went to "Kenya" and saw that there were thirty-seven languages. Tom found Luo and emailed it to James from his phone. A day later Tom received the following email:

Tom was only a digital handshake away from the Luo villages of Kenya.

> *That video is great. I had watched the English version before, but I was really fascinated watching the Luo version. I have sent the link to a number of friends and relatives here in the US and back at home in Kenya. Thanks very much.*
> *– James*

Tom was only a digital handshake away from the Luo

villages of Kenya – much easier than flying all the way to Nairobi.

In case you are doubting whether people in such places as rural Africa watch videos on the internet, let's look at some current information:

- There are 3.5 billion internet users in the world today – nearly half of the world's people.[17]

- More than 4 billion videos are watched on YouTube each day, and 80% are outside North America.[18]

- More people in the world own a cell phone than a toothbrush.[19]

- 70% of the global population will have smart phones by 2020.[20]

I have personally observed people watching full-length movies on mobile phones on four continents. When I see them, I think of the four reels of 16 mm film weighing over 40 lbs. that we needed to show the *JESUS* film when it was distributed in 1980, not to mention the heavy projector and the screen used to show them. The last thirty-five years have seen drastic changes in the transfer of visual images.

When my family and I moved to Central Asia twenty years ago, we already had the *JESUS* film on video tape cassette, the pinnacle of analog technology developed in Japan to make film available to home TVs. At that time, our *JESUS* film team members *only* needed to carry a VHS (Video Home System) cassette, a VCR (video cassette recorder), and a bulky television in order to show the *JESUS* film.

Then we had the digital revolution. "Digital" refers to the storage of information using binary code – on/off switches represented by the digits 0 and 1. When computers made it possible to store and to quickly read massive amounts of information, all stored as zeroes and ones, the digital age began. Soon, our film could be stored on the most primitive form of digital disc, a VCD (video compact disc); actually, it required two VCDs, since the VCD could store only about 75 minutes of content.

Then came the DVD (digital video disc or digital versatile disc). Since 1996, millions of people have seen Jesus speak to them in their own heart language through DVDs played on home TVs and computers. For the 35th anniversary of the *JESUS* film, we cleaned up the film frame by frame, created an entirely new symphonic score and sound track, and created an HD version of the film. Literally millions of *JESUS* film DVDs have been distributed around the world in all kinds of ways, and stories constantly come into our office of the changed lives that have resulted.

Distraught over her broken engagement, Dara was determined to take her own life. She walked to a nearby park, where she noticed a booklet and DVD on a bench. At first she thought someone had forgotten them. Then she saw a note under the booklet. Reaching for it, she read: "This is a gift for you. I got it free; I give it free. The content of the DVD and book changed my life, and it can change yours as well. Do not lose this opportunity . . . Hope will return into your life." The note overwhelmed her, and as she looked more closely at the items, she discovered a copy of one of the Gospels and a *JESUS* film DVD. Dara quickly returned home, went to her room, and started to watch *JESUS*. While watching the movie, she began to cry. Her parents, concerned, entered her room. They, too, began watching the film. By the end of the movie, all three wept tears of joy, and all three chose to follow Jesus Christ that day. Although Christianity is illegal in their country, through Christian broadcasting via satellite, Dara and her parents began growing in their faith. Eventually her younger brother also came to Christ, and today their home serves as a small church.[21]

> The police were watching the *JESUS* film.

In a closed country, a *JESUS* film team prayed and made a bold plan to give out *JESUS* DVDs, Bibles, and other Christian books in thirty-five villages. At first, they were dismayed at the lack of opportunities to distribute the materials. Then one afternoon they were stopped by police with guns drawn. As the police searched the car, they said, "Yes, these are the ones!" and brought them to the police station, counted the materials, and locked them up downstairs. To the team's surprise, about an hour later, they heard sounds from upstairs – the police were watching the *JESUS* film. "Hallelujah!" the team rejoiced downstairs, but then they heard the head man come in upstairs. The sound of the film stopped. However, as soon as he left, they could hear the police resume watching the film. The next day, the decision was made to release the team, along with their materials. As the team was getting ready to leave, two policemen came up and asked if they could have a DVD. Then another policeman came to the team. "You gave a DVD to my friend; may I have one, too?" Likewise, ten other policemen did the same thing. The team was able to give out all 250 DVDs and all the books to the policemen at the station.[22]

Now we have the ability to stream and download video over the internet, and the Jesus Film Project created the Arclight Digital media platform from which we can serve over 75,000 videos in over 1,500 languages on demand anywhere in the world. The Arclight platform supports over a dozen video apps, including our own Jesus Film Project app.

A Cru staff member serving at Disney World in Orlando told us, "The Jesus Film app is such an amazing tool for ministry, as I regularly share the gospel with many international cast members at Disney. I remember one time I used it to show the *JESUS* film to one of my students from China. It was such an amazing experience! My student was so inspired when he heard Jesus speak in [his heart language]. He told me he had never felt so close to God as at that moment. The feeling when you hear Jesus talking in your language is amazing."[23]

For those who do not yet have a smartphone or access to the internet, we have the micro SD card, a small disc the size of your little fingernail, designed to play data on a mobile device such as a feature phone, or "dumb" phone, which does not have internet connectivity. We can get eight languages of the *JESUS* film on a micro SD card!

The increased portability of communication technology is a special blessing in areas of the world where followers of Jesus suffer persecution. A dear servant of the Lord in West Africa recently sent us a short video report of his ongoing service among the villages terrorized by Muslim extremists.

God is bringing the great joy of knowing His love to many people.

He reported that he is not able to show the *JESUS* film openly in churches because Muslim extremists will burn down the church building if it is used for that purpose. But his team is going house to house showing the *JESUS* film to people in their heart languages on mobile phones, and God is bringing the great joy of knowing His love to many people.

Another report came to us from Yantu, a West African university student who had received a tablet loaded with his area's languages of the *JESUS* film. He and five friends shared the tablet, taking turns using it for evangelism by showing the *JESUS* film and a follow-up film series called *Walking With Jesus, Africa.* Tragically, terrorists attacked his university and burned it down. As Yantu fled for his life, the only possession he had time to grab was the tablet. While hiding out in the bush, he continued to use it to show the *JESUS* film. Eventually he made his way to another city, still with tablet in hand. He reported, "Despite how they [the terrorists] did everything, the tablet is here. Why? The simple reason is because the tablet is mobile. Anyway, I find myself now, even homeless – I think I am privileged to share, I'm privileged to share with the tablet."[24] No home, but a tablet; what a hero!

This is the age of visual story. Television, Facebook, YouTube, Instagram – these are the most prominent examples of a global phenomenon. Most people prefer watching to reading.

A generation ago, scholars and missionaries began to focus on "oral learners," those people in the world who, because of illiteracy or other factors, learn primarily or exclusively through oral, not textual, means. They devised new methods for teaching in primitive cultures and others who were oral learners. Today many use recent communication technology to communicate the good news of Jesus to oral cultures. Those who cannot read the Bible still have it available to them in the form of audio Bibles and Bible-based films.

At the same time, recent technology has brought visual story to the forefront of communication for the most media-sophisticated people in the world – the wired and connected youth of the world's cities.

Studies have shown that 80% of the world's population are oral learners![25]

Clyde Tabor of the Visual Story Network has said, "The church has been slow to adopt new forms of communication in our era of rapid change. Critical Gospel opportunities are lost . . . *the world is increasingly screen-dominated, story-oriented, and mobile-saturated."* The message remains the same; the means of communicating it are ever new. It is time for the good news to be powerfully communicated through short, compelling pieces of visual story – poignant and comic, culturally relevant – God's love communicated to everyone in the language they understand best.

It is time for a spiritual renewal to match the new renaissance of global communication. God is raising up a generation of people who will use every means to proclaim His love to every person on earth.

Chapter 5

The Answer to Every Problem

Recently, I gathered with half a million of my closest friends on the National Mall in Washington, D.C. The event was called Reset: Together 2016, and it was organized by millennials for millennials, with some of the rest of us there to cheer them on. We prayed for God to reset our own hearts, to reset our nation, and to reset the world through the good news of Jesus Christ. We prayed for those impacted by racism – both the haters and the hated. We prayed for those who were considering having abortions and for those busy with adoption and foster care. We prayed for those trapped in poverty and those deceived by wealth. We prayed for the LGBTQ community and the indigenous peoples of North America, as well as for the unevangelized peoples of the world and even Muslim terrorists. We prayed all over the political spectrum, from the right to the left, because Jesus' teaching is bigger than anybody's political agenda, and we wanted – we desperately want

– to be *His* disciples. Our theme was "Jesus Changes Everything," because He does, and He will.

I am a child of the 60s. We had our Jesus Movement, our Explo '72, and our New Evangelicalism. We brought the Western church a new form of music. I remember when any song accompanied by a guitar and not found in the hymnbook was considered radical, and the "Christian music" section of the corner bookstore was where you found Bach and Handel. We brought a new emphasis on the church as the Body of Christ rather than as an organization. Many of us were enabled by the Spirit of God to see through the superficiality of modern Western culture and were able to do counter-cultural things like boldly share about faith in Jesus and cross cultures to take His love to the world.

I arrived on the Harvard campus in 1970, the fall after riots over the Vietnam War and racial segregation had cancelled final exams the previous spring. I was a Jesus freak with a big red beard and jeans with torn knees. Several dozen of us Jesus followers took on Harvard secularism. We made it our goal to share the good news with everyone who would listen. I had one friend who went door-to-door and shared with every person in his residential house.

The biggest challenge we faced was being relevant. Everyone told us Christianity was not relevant. In fact, no religion was relevant. We were the generation of the "Secular City" where God was dead and only economics and politics mattered. Being a follower of Jesus was not radical enough.

Now, as I look back on the certainties about the

irrelevance of religion in the 60s, I have to laugh. Religion not relevant? By the mid 80s, my Harvard professor Harvey Cox, author of *The Secular City,* was among the first to prophesy, in his book *Religion in the Secular City,* that both radical Islam and conservative Christianity would play major roles in years to come.[26]

Today the secular experts are scrambling to understand how the religion of a desert prophet could be the most relevant topic on the world scene. When I tell

They may charge me with insanity, but not irrelevancy.

my old secular college friends that my years sharing the good news of Jesus with Muslims were an expression of the only force radical enough to counter the power of Islam, they do not charge me with being irrelevant. They may charge me with insanity, but not irrelevancy.

One of my dear friends in Central Asia is Makhmud, formerly trained as a terrorist at a camp in Afghanistan. He returned to his home country when he heard that his sister had become a Christian. He intended to kill the *JESUS* film team leader who had shared with her about Jesus, and force his sister back to Islam. He asked his sister if he could accompany her to a meeting of her Christian friends, where he thought he would finalize his plan to kill the leader. He quietly sat in the meeting, and something totally unexpected happened to him. The evident love and openness of the group arrested his attention. He sensed a presence he had never felt before. After attending several such meetings, Makhmud gave his own life to Jesus, and I got to know him as he risked his life to share his newfound relationship with Jesus with his Muslim friends.

Makhmud is not the only former extremist Muslim I knew in Central Asia. That is why the Boston Marathon bombing hit me so hard. Tamerlan and Dzhokhar Tsarnaev, the young men who carried out that terrible act, were from Central Asia. Tamerlan was named for Timur the Lame (Amir Timur), whose larger-than-life statue loomed over the central square of the city in which we lived for ten years. I knew lots of young men like the Tsarnaevs in that region, torn between their desire for the financial and cultural success of the modern world and their attachment to the religion and resentment of their ancestors. Some turn one way, some another. Many fought with the Taliban against the USA in Afghanistan. I also know many who have become followers of Jesus Christ and are leaders in spiritual movements in some very difficult places. They have been transformed just like Paul in the Bible, who turned from persecutor to apostle.

How sad it was to read the words of Tamerlan Tsarnaev as reported in the aftermath of his murderous act: "I don't have a single American friend. I don't understand them." We American Christians (rightly) give substantial attention to sending people halfway around the world to reach young men like the Tsarnaev brothers with the love of Jesus Christ, yet we often fail to realize: They are coming to us! Are they coming to do us harm or are they coming to be transformed by the love of Jesus Christ? Will they strike at our hearts, or will Jesus touch theirs? The answer to those questions, in part, is up to you and me. Jesus is the solution to the problem of radical Islamic terrorism.

What about the economic solutions the political left was promoting in the 60s? The Soviet Union, for many the model socialist republic, has fallen under its own weight. Paul Eshleman, founding director of the Jesus Film Project, tells the story of showing the film in one of the former Soviet capital cities immediately after the dissolution of the USSR. At the end of the film there is a direct call to personal faith in Christ, and Paul's team wondered how this would be received by people who had been indoctrinated in atheism for seventy years. Paul decided to let it play through without comment and see what would happen. To his shock and delight, everyone in the packed theater stood to their feet to receive Jesus Christ as Lord and Savior. One man said through tears, "These have been the best two hours of my life." Another gasped, "We need this film more than bread."[27]

Political systems are not the answer. Jesus is the answer. It is clear that even our American system has not brought justice for all. As American Christians, we need to continue to humbly repent of *our own* sins and seek God for His mercy. We must recognize that the only salt and light in American life are the followers of Jesus, living lives based on His truth and empowered by His Spirit. Christians are all over the political spectrum on questions of economic justice, some emphasizing the parts of Jesus' teaching that demand compassion for the poor and oppressed, and others the parts that emphasize personal stewardship and work ethic. We need to respect one another and recognize that our different gifts and callings are complementary, not contradictory. We need to listen more and talk less, seeking to genuinely understand the variety of perspectives that race, ethnicity, and personal history have granted us. We need to love one another and others with real heartfelt empathy. This is the way of Jesus. He is the answer to the gulf between the rich and the poor.

Jesus transcends class. A non-Christian woman living in a Middle Eastern country received a gift of a multi-language DVD of *JESUS*. When she saw that one of the film versions on the DVD was in an East African country's language, she offered it to her house helper who was from that country. The young

Jesus transcends class.

African woman watched the film and was in tears by the end of it. She went to her employer and asked her to explain the gospel and teach her how to become a follower of Jesus. The Middle Eastern woman did not know what to do, so she began watching the Arabic version of *JESUS* on the same DVD. She was so moved by the story of Jesus that she wanted to follow Him, as well! Together, the two women bowed and prayed to receive Christ as their Savior. Following this life-changing event, they contacted a church for copies of the New Testament to continue learning and growing in Christ. They became sisters, despite the difference in their social status.[28]

The journey with Jesus always begins with personal transformation. People constantly send to the Jesus

Film Project stories of precious people whom Jesus has set free.

Freed from alcoholism

Adela walked down the street, inviting villagers to a Christian gathering. Soon, he began sharing the good news with a woman standing in her yard. Overhearing their conversation, a drunken man, I'll call him Sergey, stumbled to them. Tossing his cigarette aside, he admitted, "I am a very sinful man. I have many flaws. I'm a bad man. What must I do?" Adela told the man to repent. He responded, "But I'm drunk all the time. Will God receive me?" Adela explained that God would hear him if he was honest with God and prayed for forgiveness for his sins. The man agreed to pray. Laying his hand on the man, Adela prayed that the man would open his heart to Jesus.

Upon finishing the prayer, the man exclaimed, "What did you do to me? When you put your hand on my shoulder I felt something change inside me." The man no longer felt the effects of alcohol. Adela gave the man a copy of the New Testament and arranged to visit his home the next day to explain more about Jesus. During the follow-up visit, eleven of the man's relatives also indicated decisions for Christ.[29]

In the same region of the world, a young woman we'll call Luba lay crumpled in the middle of a snow-covered street, passed out from drinking. Feodora approached and helped her to stand and walk home. "Feodora told me only God could help me! But I didn't believe in anything at that time," said Luba.

Like so many destitute women in this region, Luba's parents died when she was a teenager. Her brother, who drank a lot, raised Luba with little supervision. By age seventeen, she had her own son to care for. "As a result, I turned up on the bottom of society," said Luba, now twenty-three.

Feodora invited Luba to her home that cold winter day, and the next afternoon they met and watched *Magdalena,* the women's version of the *JESUS* film. "It was about a woman like me. Society had turned away from her, and only Jesus was able to help her." Afterwards, Feodora invited Luba to a *Rivka* study group; *Rivka* is a discipleship film series created for women. During one of the lessons, Luba prayed and accepted Christ. The women from the group provided Luba and her young son with clothes and food. Encouraged, Luba showed the *Rivka* series to a friend she used to drink with. "We try to study the lessons, and I can see that it is difficult for her," she said. "But God is working in her heart."

Now, Luba looks to the future with optimism. "I know that with God I can survive any difficulties that may come, and He will help me through His children, who surround me. Praise God that He didn't leave me to freeze and die in the snow, but sent Feodora to help me."[30]

Every evening Pa Sorie and several friends met at a village bar in West Africa to drink palm wine. Many nights ended in drunkenness. One evening as he walked home, he came upon a *JESUS* film showing in his language of Mende. He stopped to watch. The message moved him so much that he gave his life to

Christ. *JESUS* film team members met with him for the next six days, taking him through follow-up lessons. At the end of the follow-up, he received a Proclaimer, a solar-powered audio Bible player developed by a ministry called Faith Comes by Hearing. Some friends noticed his absence and decided to visit him. When they arrived at his home, he was listening to his Proclaimer, and they joined him. A *JESUS* film team member explained to the men what they were hearing. That day, Pa Sorie's friends made decisions to follow Jesus Christ. This small group of men no longer visits the bar to drink wine, but in the evenings they meet at Pa Sorie's home for a listening Bible study, much to the delight of his wife and children.[31]

Freed from addiction to drugs

JESUS Film Harvest Partners, a ministry of the Church of the Nazarene, received a report from their team in Ecuador: "Several years ago, we planted a new church using the *JESUS* film. The church is growing and has purchased property. This is significant since the church is located in a low-income area riddled with drug use, especially among the young people. We have seen God at work. As the Bible says, *Where sin increased, grace increased all the more* (Romans 5:20)."

Many people are coming to the church and finding Jesus. Andrea started using drugs when she was only twelve years old. When she came to the church, she was totally transformed by the Word of God. Now, she is a children's Sunday school teacher and assists in the services. Andrea is a living example of the power of God."[32]

Freed from sexual addiction

"I was not able to change my life," said the twenty-year-old Nicaraguan. "I have tried drugs, alcohol, and sexual promiscuity. My family gave me warnings and advice about my lifestyle. I did not listen. I would get mad and shout at them to not meddle in my affairs. In my heart, I knew they were right in all they said; I just was not able to change. Tonight, I watched the *JESUS* film and I realized it is possible to change by allowing Jesus to be the absolute owner of my life. When the team asked if there were those who wanted to serve Christ, there was a fight inside me. I just did not want to go, but I knew Christ was my only hope for change. I struggled for several minutes, and at last I went forward confessing my sins. I accepted Him as my Savior and asked His help to make me different. For the first time, I feel peace. I have confidence in Christ that I will succeed in overcoming all my addictions. I am excited about my future."[33]

Freed from the oppression of demons

This report is like many we have received through the years from joyful Christian workers. "We used the projector to show the *JESUS* film in a village. . . . Many people watched the movie. One particular family believed in Jesus. This family had been under the dominion of evil spirits for several years. While they watched the movie and saw how Jesus cast out demons, a miracle happened. The evil spirits left that family immediately. I (a film team member) saw it happening in front of me and praised God for delivering this family. All glory to my Jesus. There are five members in that family. . . . All of them have received Jesus Christ as their personal Savior. Now they are attending the church and growing in Christ."[34]

Our Wesleyan partner, JESUS Film Global Partners, sent us the story of Amend, husband and father of three, who had been possessed by an evil spirit for five years. Many of his actions were those of a madman: throwing things, beating people in the village, and running around the village as though insane. His wife was forced to keep him tied up by rope in his home, binding his hands and legs. She also needed to dress him and feed him. This was a tremendous burden on the family. People of the village suggested that his family take him to the witch doctors; he was taken to more than fifteen, but they could do nothing for him. Then his family took him to well-known medical doctors, but they had no answers. Amend and his family lost all hope. One day the JESUS film team arrived in Amend's village to show the film, and he came to see the film that night. The many miracles of Christ captivated him, including His casting out of demons. Amend believed he would be cured if he placed his faith in Christ, and as the film team prayed over him, God did deliver him. Amend now is learning to walk in Christ and is being trained as a follower of Jesus.[35]

> Amend believed he would be cured if he placed his faith in Christ.

In a small village in a South Asian country, Pema, a teenager, displayed signs of demon possession for nine months. *JESUS* film team member, Joseph, his wife, and two other Campus Crusade for Christ staff members came to Pema's home and prayed for her for seven days. Each day they saw improvement, bit by bit. On the seventh day she arose, then prepared and served tea to her parents and the others. Her family was amazed! When they saw Pema's deliverance through the prayers of Christians, they said, "The god we serve is really not God. They are devil. So we want to get away." They piled together all the statues of their gods, poured gas on them, and burned them. Pema and all her family, seven people in all, chose to follow Christ. Others in their village saw the change in Pema and heard of her deliverance. Joseph showed the *JESUS* film in the village, and many more received Christ. Eventually everyone in the entire village – twenty-five families (sixty-five people) – became Christians and formed one church. Joseph continues to teach them and recently baptized thirty-two adults in that village.[36]

Freed from despair

"My daughter was a human sacrifice," said Naru from Benin. "I sacrificed my five-year-old daughter to evil. My desire was to grow rich. This failed, as the people of my town turned me over to the police. I was sentenced to ten years in prison, and my wife divorced me. A month ago, while serving my seventh year in prison, a pastor showed me the *JESUS* film on a laptop computer. I had lost all hope until I saw the film. I repented, accepting the love of Christ. I cried for three days. Jesus transformed me and forgave me. Now, I lead a prayer group in prison and am the pastor of evangelism. The Lord saved me to serve Him; when I get out of prison, I will become a pastor to lead lost souls to Jesus."[37]

Freed from sickness

Anna, who lives in a country where there are not yet many followers of Jesus, was bedridden for three years and completely unable to walk. She heard of plans to show the *JESUS* film in her village and wanted very much to see it, so friends carried her to the film location on a wooden cart. As she watched the miracles portrayed in the film, she felt something working in her life. She cried out to the Lord, "If You are God, heal me." As the movie ended and everyone began to walk home, they were amazed to see Anna walking with them! Film team members went to her home, prayed with her, and shared the gospel. At that time, she received Christ as her Lord and Savior. Seeing the miracle in her life, her husband, a successful businessman in the liquor business, also received Christ and then chose to leave his business. Anna could not remain quiet about what happened to her. She began to share her faith with family members and friends, many of whom came to know the Lord as a result of her testimony. A pastor in Anna's village was so encouraged by her story that he began using the *JESUS* film in his ministry. After using the film, God blessed his ministry in phenomenal ways. He personally baptized more than 5,000 people, and 70 churches have been planted![38] God does not heal everyone immediately; only in heaven will all be made whole. But he heals some miraculously in order to show the reality of His promise to heal everyone who comes to Him.

Freed from idol worship

Fear gripped the residents in a village in Ghana where idol worship held sway over the hearts of 70 percent of the population. Many, especially among the youth, desired to know more about Christ, but the fear of being stigmatized and having their homes ransacked held them in check. This inspired James, a ministry worker, to share his faith in Christ with the youth. Earlier he had seen *Walking With Jesus*, a five-part follow-up film series contextualized for Africans to help new believers grow in their relationships with Christ. One episode specifically deals with idol worship. James felt that this film was also a great tool for evangelism. Together with twelve university students, James showed *Walking With Jesus*, while 280 residents, youth and parents, quietly watched. The film depicts what happens when a person abandons the practice of idol worship and turns to worship the one true God. At the film's conclusion, ninety people indicated decisions to receive Christ, and many others renewed their commitment to Him. James said, "Since then, I have been using this episode often at my first shows, especially when I enter communities where idol worship is very high."[39]

We westerners do not worship idols in the traditional sense, but who can deny that we have made idols of wealth, comfort, and control. Some of the most radical

American Christians I know are those who have been set free from these idols and who give generously to the cause of sharing the good news of Jesus with everyone. They are obeying Jesus, who said, *Do not lay up for yourselves treasures on earth, where moth and rust destroy and where thieves break in and steal, but lay up for yourselves treasures in heaven, where neither moth nor rust destroys and where thieves do not break in and steal. For where your treasure is, there your heart will be also* (Matthew 6:19-21 NKJV). He later said, *If you want to be perfect, go, sell your possessions and give to the poor, and you will have treasure in heaven. Then come, follow me* (Matthew 19:21). I have seen wealthy men and women give nearly all they have to see the Great Commission fulfilled.

> The most radical thing we can do is introduce a person to Jesus Christ.

Some might object that their money might have been better spent feeding people or providing water or shelter. Many of them have given to those things as well, and have done so in the name of Jesus, who told us to care for those in need. But they consider their giving to transform people from within to be their most radical action. Why?

We've all heard the old proverb, "Give a man a fish and he'll eat for a day; teach him to fish and he'll eat for a lifetime." Many have discovered that our most benevolent humanitarian efforts never escape the curse of paternalism. Many have learned to recognize "when helping hurts." The most radical thing we can do is introduce a person to Jesus Christ. She or he immediately becomes our sister or brother, a full-fledged co-heir of all the riches of God in Christ. The same Spirit that moved us to love now lives in her or him. The same power to call on Almighty God for help, for oneself and for others, is at her or his disposal. We become fellow sojourners in the path of Jesus. And, after forty-five additional years of life experience, I ask you: What could be more radical than that?

Chapter 6

The Fulfillment of
Every Longing

Within each of us there is a God-shaped hole. Throughout the centuries, the wisest of men have testified to this. Solomon said, "He has put eternity in the human heart." Saint Augustine echoed, "You have made us for yourself, and our hearts are restless, until they can find rest in you." The French philosopher Blaise Pascal wrote, "What else does this craving, and this helplessness, proclaim but that there was once in man a true happiness, of which all that now remains is the empty print and trace? This he tries in vain to fill with everything around him, seeking in things that are not there the help he cannot find in those that are, though none can help, since this infinite abyss can be filled only with an infinite and immutable object; in other words, by God himself."[40]

The great religious traditions in the world are full of

expressions of this ache for God, this longing for holiness, this craving for acceptance, this need for ultimate purpose. We see it in the attempt of Muslims to bring righteousness to the earth through jihad, in the journey of the Buddhist monk seeking to be liberated from suffering, and even in the rituals of the animist seeking to control forces that cannot be fully understood.

Those who are not given to religion or philosophy cry out all the same, in all sorts of ways. We cry out for meaning, we long for acceptance, we crave respect, we want to be made whole.

Jesus is the fulfillment of every longing. So many of the stories that come to us reflect this multi-faceted truth. He arranges circumstances **Jesus is the fulfillment** to bring people to Himself, He **of every longing.** reveals truth to give meaning to their lives, and He fulfills people's longing with His own loving presence.

Keung was abandoned at a railway station in an Asian country as a two-year-old with a physical disability. He grew up in an orphanage and struggled with feelings of rejection. As an adult, he participated in a workshop at a Christian counseling center. When one of the center's consultants gave Keung a copy of *JESUS*, he immediately returned home to watch the film. A few weeks later, one of the workshop participants asked Keung how he manages the struggles he faces each day living with his disability. Keung replied, "Compared to Jesus, the suffering I endure is nothing!" He explained his source of his newfound perspective: "I will often read the Bible and watch the disc of *JESUS*. I do my best to become a blessing to others." Keung found acceptance and meaning in a personal relationship with Jesus.[41]

Bataar came to Christ as a first-year college student in China when some fellow students showed him the *JESUS* film. He too was an orphan. "My life was full of sorrow, loneliness, bitterness, and separation, but after all these sufferings, God gave me friends that I never had before." Later that year, Bataar participated in a mission trip to a rural area. "It was my first time to show the *JESUS* film and share the gospel. . . . It was such a wonderful experience to witness their response during the showing of the film. They were amazed by God's love. . . . Several made decisions to become Jesus' followers." Now as Bataar completes his senior year of college, he senses God's calling. "I have a desire to prepare many disciples – disciples who are willing to live missionally. Even though I do not have parents, God has chosen me and many other students to bring the lost to Him." Bataar found belonging and purpose in Jesus.[42]

Today, millions are suffering the humiliation of homelessness as refugees, many of them previously respectable citizens of their homeland, wrenched from their secure places in society by war, persecution, and terrorism. According to the United Nations' refugee agency, there are more displaced people today than at any time in human history.

In a refugee camp in a Middle Eastern country, a church-planting team met a twenty-one-year-old woman whom I'll call Khawla. She showed up at a showing of the film *Magdalena*, a version of the *JESUS* film made especially for women that includes scenes from the Gospels showing Jesus' interaction with women. When the film ended, her questions began. She had never heard about Jesus before and was shocked by His miracles, by His respect for women, and by the fact that He died for her. As she left the film showing, Khawla asked for a Bible. One week later, she returned to the center and told the team she was reading the Bible. "What must I do to become a Christian?" she asked. "Do I need to declare that I'm a Christian to all my family and neighbors? Should I take off my veil?"

The staff members responded, "It is enough to pray to Jesus and ask Him into your life."

Khawla began to watch the film series *Rivka*, created to answer the questions of women from Muslim backgrounds who want to become followers of Jesus. When she came to an episode that talked about teen marriage, it brought to the surface Khawla's own painful story. Through her tears, she shared that her father had forced her to marry when she was fifteen years old, and that her husband was very aggressive. As she shared her story with the team, she confided, "The way Jesus shows respect to women, that's one of the most attractive parts of the Christian faith." Khawla found in Jesus the honor and respect for which her heart longed.[43]

The film *Magdalena*, which touched Khawla so deeply, was conceived in the heart of Willie Erasmus, one of our Jesus Film Project staff members. One day, when Willie was involved in a distribution of humanitarian aid in Afghanistan, he noticed a group of women in their blue burkas, cowering in a vacant building to one side. They all had small children with them. A bearded man with a stick was guarding them, and when they spoke to one another, the guard would beat them.

"Who are those women?" Willie asked.

"Oh, those are the widows," he was told. "If there is anything left at the end, they'll get something."

Willie's heart began to break, and he wondered, "How can these women understand the love of God when He came to earth as a man, if this is how men treat them?" He continued to be haunted by this question, until he had the idea of making a movie from the Gospels focused on Jesus' expressions of love for women.

God has used the film *Magdalena* to touch the hearts of millions of women who experienced shame from their culture or their family experience.

In one northern African village, a woman we'll call Asma became suspicious; she knew something was happening in a particular house where many women met regularly, and she was very angry. She suspected the meetings were attended by believers, but she wasn't sure. She wanted to find out, but was so angry she dared not speak with them. Whenever Asma saw one of the women on the road, she would curse and swear, calling them prostitutes and betrayers of her family's religion. However, they always greeted her pleasantly, even though they never received a greeting in return.

Later, Asma's husband was unfaithful to her, and everyone in the village heard about it. This brought shame upon her. One day on the road, she passed one of the "Magdalena" women, but instead of cursing, she hung her head in shame, wanting to walk past unnoticed.

One of the women walked up to her and greeted her. She said, "We care about you and want to talk to you." Asma burst into tears and they embraced. The women took her to their home and comforted her. They also demonstrated love and acceptance. Later, after watching *Magdalena*, Asma realized this was what she had missed all her life. She became a follower of Jesus and experienced release from her shame.[44]

Much of the world's religion reflects the fear that we all feel in the face of the unknown, the powerlessness we feel, and the lack of control of the circumstances of our lives. We long for control and power, but Jesus quenches this longing by calling us to trust Him and to surrender to His control and power.

During a 2014 *JESUS* film showing in a mountain-side village twenty-five miles north of Port-au-Prince, Haiti, a young woman watched with intensity. The Holy Spirit opened the heart of this nineteen-year-old to accept His offer of life. When *JESUS* film team members met with her the next day for follow-up, they discovered she was not the typical adherent to ancient superstitions and worship of false gods. She confessed she had been preparing to become a *Mambo* – a voodoo priestess. Now filled with the zeal of a sincere commitment to Christ, she burned all of the handmade idols in her home. Praise the Lord for giving this precious young woman the courage to let go and trust in Him as the

> We long for control and power, but Jesus quenches this longing by calling us to trust Him and to surrender to His control and power.

first teenager in her community to reject witchcraft and live for Jesus.[45]

Historically, religion has answered the human longing to understand the universe and to know the future. The Mayan religion included astronomical research that was centuries ahead of its time in understanding the movement of the planets and the calculation of the calendar. Some predicted the future based on these calculations. You may recall that some were saying the world would end according to the Mayan calendar on December 21, 2012. Instead, what began in 2012 was a significant spiritual movement among the Mayan people of the Yucatan Peninsula, as a group called the Message for Mayans, led by Erik and Elizabeth Groves and Gamaliel Gonzalez, began to show *Magdalena* and *The Story of Jesus for Children* (a children's version of the *JESUS* film) in rural villages. The team knew they were onto something early on, when in one village, 260 people watched the film and some 250 of them indicated they wanted to trust Jesus as Savior. For the last four years, the team has visited two villages each weekend with similar results every week. For tens of thousands of Mayans, instead of the world ending, their new lives in Christ are just beginning.[46]

The religious traditions of Asia reflect a serious grappling with the human condition, the sense we all feel that something is not as it should be.

In a crowd of approximately one hundred people watching the *JESUS* film in a country in South Asia sat a Buddhist monk. He watched the film very intently and heard Jesus say that He is the Way, and that He could offer reconciliation with God the creator: "Whoever believes Me, believes My Father." When the film ended, he came to the film team and started talking about the Path of Buddhism. They explained to him that no matter what anyone does, no one can gain salvation by works. They shared with him that Jesus is the one who hears our voice, speaks to us, sees and walks, and helps us in our every work. Their words pierced his heart, and the monk, an honest and sincere man, told the team he wanted to accept Jesus as his God and Savior.[47]

So many people know that God exists, but they do not have a personal relationship with Him; yet their hearts long for that relationship. This is certainly true among Muslims. God is revealing to many Muslims in dreams and visions that Jesus is the way to know Him personally.

One hot summer afternoon the sun was beating down on a volunteer distributor of *JESUS* film packets at a port city in France. Jamie, the volunteer, wished she could be somewhere other than standing at her assigned spot where it was so uncomfortable. Then suddenly, another volunteer brought a North African man to Jamie because she spoke French and he wanted to talk about something. Jamie attentively listened as the man told an amazing story. He had a dream in which he was in a graveyard. He saw a man in a white robe with a rod in one hand and a book in the other saying, "Come, come!" The man said he knew this was Jesus and that Jesus is God. After listening to his dream, Jamie shared the gospel in French, and he prayed to receive Christ as Savior. God engineered the circumstances of the man's dream with a divine portside encounter, because God loved him and wanted to fulfill the longing of his heart to know Him.[48]

As a part of the follow-up after a *JESUS* film showing, the local pastor in an African village organized an open-air service for discussion with those who had watched the film. Ruha, an elder in this Islamic community and a sincere seeker of God, explained that he struggled with the idea that Jesus could be the Son of God; however, he was very impressed with Jesus. The conviction of the Holy Spirit was clearly at work in Ruha as he confessed that although he often criticized Christians, secretly he admired their lifestyle and faith. He listened carefully as the preacher clearly shared how to know Jesus, and he accepted the message of grace and truth. Immediately, he testified of experiencing God's love and peace, which he had never experienced before. He exclaimed, "I am happy that I found the right Savior, even at the age of seventy-five!"[49]

Our ultimate longing for eternity will be met only when we reach heaven, but the Holy Spirit is given to followers of Jesus as a foretaste of the age to come. What a joy to see the Holy Spirit working around the world to reveal Jesus to precious people from every part of the world, fulfilling their hearts' longings.

Chapter 7

Everyone is Free to Decide

Shortly after my family moved to Central Asia, one of our friends was trying to make sense of the stories we were sending home about persecution of those who came to faith in Christ and having informants in all my university classes, being followed, having our phone tapped, betrayal and denial by some professing believers. My friend asked, "Tell me, is there any model in the Bible for ministry in a closed country?"

I thought about it for a moment and realized how alive the book of Acts was becoming to me day by day. I answered, "The whole New Testament is a model for ministry in a closed country – *the Roman Empire was closed*!" Opposition, persecution, betrayal – these are not exceptional circumstances for the follower of Jesus; they are the normal Christian life. The American experience of religious freedom, where Christians are a majority and we think it is our right to be respected – that is the exception.

One thing I learned from over a decade of living in Muslim countries is that I don't need cultural authority to live a powerful Christian life and to do my job of working toward the fulfillment of the Great Commission. I can show the love of Jesus Christ and share His good news everywhere, whether or not the laws of the land or the traditions of the culture support me in doing so.

The Bible does instruct us to pray for good government. *I urge, then, first of all, that petitions, prayers, intercession and thanksgiving be made for all people – for kings and all those in authority, that we may live peaceful and quiet lives in all godliness and holiness. This is good, and pleases God our Savior, who wants all people to be saved and to come to a knowledge of the truth,* writes the apostle Paul (1 Timothy 2:1-4). But we must see that the context of this prayer is our prayer for *all people* and God's heart for *all people* to be saved and come to know Him. Good government is one means to an end, and not the end in itself. The power of government should never be used in a way that drives people from God or holds people back from Him.

God is in favor of free choice. He showed this from the beginning when He allowed the first man and woman to walk away from Him in disobedience. He showed it most clearly when He allowed His own Son to be rejected and killed. He has shown it throughout the entire age of the church as He allows His own people to be persecuted. He shows it in the existential moment that each and every person must face, as each and every person must decide, whether to resist God in pride or humbly accept Him as Lord.

This is a difficult idea to understand – how an all-powerful God would choose to restrain that power and allow humans to make choices.

The average Muslim, for example, does not understand this. There is no separation of church and state in Islam. The state should enforce God's law; this *is* right religion in the minds of most of the world's Muslims. That is why I've been asked so many times by young Muslims why America exports the filth we see in the world's open markets; they see America as a Christian country, so they associate these things with Christianity. I tell them God gives people choices. There are both godly people and bad people in America, followers of Jesus and those who do not follow Him. God is not judging the world yet. He is allowing the freedom to offer to everyone in the world the chance to repent of their sin and return to Him. As followers of Jesus, we should be offering this good news to everyone, everywhere.

> As followers of Jesus, we should be offering this good news to everyone, everywhere.

Yet more than half of the countries of the world do not allow religious freedom. Christians are persecuted in 105 of the world's 196 countries. It has been estimated that more Christians have died as martyrs in the twentieth and twenty-first centuries than during the previous nineteen centuries combined.[50] What should be our response to this reality?

- We should understand that this is the normal Christian life. The evangelization of the world and the persecution of the church will always go on together.

After my wife and I were attacked in Central Asia, we lay alongside each other in a hospital in Europe. Elizabeth was in a hospital bed, her head swollen to twice its normal size. I was on a rickety folding chair, having refused admission to the hospital so I could stay at her side – I would have been assigned to a different ward. We decided to process our trauma by reading Scripture, and we decided to study Paul's life as inspiration. As we read Acts and 2 Corinthians, we counted eleven times that Paul had undergone traumatic events at least as serious as ours. We looked at each other, and with our strange shared sense of humor, both said at the same time, "That's one! Ten more to go."

- We should be wise in the way we present the good news. It is one thing to suffer for Jesus; it is another to suffer for our own stupidity. We must learn to be sensitive to the Holy Spirit and listen to experienced believers.

- We should do what we can to promote religious liberty around the world and to stand with our sisters and brothers who are being persecuted. Many fine organizations like Open Doors, Voice of the Martyrs, and International

Christian Concern are helping the people of God remember those who suffer for their faith.[51]

Many stories of victory in the midst of persecution come to our Jesus Film Project office:

Khamal was revered as a leader in his East African village, and he held the key to the mosque built on the land he had donated. Unbeknownst to him, his two daughters had become believers after watching the *JESUS* film and were praying for him to become a follower of Jesus, as well. After a film team showed the *JESUS* film for two consecutive nights in his village, the religious leaders took action. They approached the location of the film showing on the third night, intent on driving away or killing the film team members. They succeeded in interrupting the film, but miraculously, no one was hurt.

Despite these efforts, many who responded to *JESUS* on the first two nights joined Khamal's daughters in what was once a small Bible study group. The group rejoiced when the Lord answered their prayers and Khamal finally joined them. After a time, he renounced his Muslim religion and led his family to join him in a church service where he publicly committed his life to Jesus. He responded to the repeated efforts by Muslim leaders to win him back by saying, "Christ gave me peace of mind, which I have never experienced in my entire life." What was once only a struggling handful of followers is now a thriving community of faith.[52]

In West Africa, a teacher of Islam who was always ready to fight for his religion regularly provoked a group of Christian students. Then a friend invited him to watch the Creole translation of the *JESUS* film. The compassion and love of Jesus struck the teacher, especially Jesus' interactions with Zacchaeus and the dying thief on the cross. He remarked that such acts of love could hardly be seen in Islam. He admitted he lacked true love and peace of mind as an ardent follower of Islam. During the call to faith at the end of the film, he came forward, repented, and gave his life to Christ. His open confession of faith brought opposition from his family and the Muslim community. He was kidnapped, tied up, and beaten, but he refused to recant. Ultimately, his family shunned him, and he continued to face unrelenting persecution. The *JESUS* film team leader invited the former teacher into his home to care for him. The team leader shared, "It's a joy to my family to help him with food, medication, clothing, and even his schooling. This kind of love is gradually attracting many of his oppressors, and even some of his family have come to Christ. Please pray with us for his growing strength and testimony."[53]

It is not only in Muslim communities that followers of Jesus suffer persecution. A man we'll call Chakor lived in a village in South Asia and came from a wealthy Hindu family. A ministry team went to this village to show the *JESUS* film in his heart language and discuss it with the villagers. The film left a strong impression on Chakor and many villagers, and after some time, Chakor professed a decision of faith in Christ. This was no easy matter for him, because his family expelled him from his house and rejected him as a family member.

Chakor married a Christian woman, and when his family found out, his brother bit him and pushed him into a well. By God's grace, Chakor survived the incident. As a result, his whole family indicated decisions for Christ and wanted to be baptized. When we last heard from him, Chakor was preparing to study in a Bible college.[54]

Of course, it is not only religious people who persecute followers of Jesus, but also political leaders who see Christianity as a threat to their power or position.

In April 2009, Pastor Hary and twenty-one church members joined Georges, a *JESUS* film team member, for a four-day mission trip to an East African city. Upon arrival in the city, the team faced disappointment because the local authority forbade any open-air showing of the *JESUS* film. Georges said, "The team took time to pray and to rely on God in the battle." Then Pastor Hary and a few of the team members met with the mayor and shared the "Four Spiritual Laws" booklet with him. God touched the mayor's heart, and he prayed to receive Christ! As a result, the doors opened for the mission trip to proceed, and the outreach ran smoothly and finished well. The *JESUS* film was shown three times with 2,600 in attendance and 1,055 people indicating decisions to become followers of Jesus. Prayer groups have been established, and a local church will continue the work there.[55]

Although Communism has lost its power in much of the world, it is still a strong ideology for many. In one Eastern European country, a Communist leader created problems for *JESUS* film workers in several villages. The situation became so difficult that the film team members said, "We have to do something about this." They met with the Communist leader and asked, "Why are you so opposed to us?"

He replied, "This is Christian religion. We don't want Christianity. I am a Communist. I will put an end to this."

Then they offered, "Why don't you watch this film? If you find anything objectionable, we will never show the film here again. We will leave this place. But on the other hand, if you don't find anything objectionable, you have to give us your word that you will not create any problems for us." Being an honest man, he agreed. They went to his home so he could have a private showing. At the end of the movie, he slowly went down on his knees and asked Christ into his life! From the next day onward, he traveled with the team members, leading them to village after village. Wherever he had influence as a former Communist leader, he started leading the way for Christ![56]

Through answers to prayer, through communication technology, through the bravery of God's people, and through the blood of the martyrs, the good news of Jesus is going to everyone, everywhere. May God grant freedom to all people in all the nations of the world to hear the good news and to come back to Him.

Chapter 8

The Work of Every Christian

The evangelization of the world is inextricably linked to the unity of the church.

Jesus prayed:

> *I do not ask for these only, but also for those who will believe in me through their word, that they may all be one, just as you, Father, are in me, and I in you, that they also may be in us, so that the world may believe that you have sent me. The glory that you have given me I have given to them, that they may be one even as we are one, I in them and you in me, that they may become perfectly one, so that the world may know that you sent me and loved them even as you loved me.* (John 17:20-23 ESV)

To put it simply, Jesus is saying that the world will believe that He was sent from God when His people are unified. The Great Commission was given by Jesus to all of His followers. It is a "Co" mission.

And yet the church of Jesus Christ seems so divided. There are the big divides between Protestants, Catholics, and Orthodox. But that is only the beginning; researchers tell us that there are more than 33,000 Christian denominations and sects. Many things divide us, including theology, history, ethnicity, race, nationality, and politics.

Is it possible to work together to proclaim Jesus Christ to a lost world?

Let me suggest some ways we can move toward unity, as we work to give everyone, everywhere a chance to hear the good news of Jesus.

Only God knows with certainty those who are His, but researchers tell us that when asked, over two billion people in the world say they are followers of Jesus Christ – over 30 percent of the world's population. Of these two billion plus, roughly 1.1 billion are Roman Catholic, 250 million are Orthodox, and the rest are Protestant.[57]

Is there any value to viewing this body of two billion Christians as a unified group when we talk about Jesus' mission, or are the issues that divide Christians so great that it is impractical to view "Christians" as a unified force for fulfilling the Great Commission of Jesus Christ?

First, let's assume that Jesus is referring in John 17 to all those who believe in Him for salvation from sin and eternal life and who have become His disciples, seeking to make Him Lord of their lives. This is the essential element of Christian unity – all who have become followers of Jesus have become one body; they have received one Spirit; they share one hope, *one Lord, one faith, one baptism, one God and Father of all who is over all through all and in all* (Ephesians 4:4-5 ESV).

Some things are more important than others – some *truths* are more important than others. The most important question is whether or not people have established a relationship with God through Jesus Christ by which their sins have been forgiven and they have received the gift of eternal life. This is the dividing line that matters more than any others. It has the most significant consequences for time and eternity. Issues of church government, mode of baptism, and beliefs about the end times are all less important than the question of reconciliation to God in Christ for time and eternity. Therefore, we must ask whether all professing Christians have come into this personal relationship with God through Jesus Christ.

This is the essential question. All who have found new life in Jesus Christ share this essential thing in common. For generations, many Christians have cooperated under this principle: "In essentials, unity; in nonessentials, liberty; in all things, charity." There are many things that all true Christians can do together, and sharing their mutual faith in Jesus with those who do not yet know Him is chief among them.

Sometimes followers of Jesus present their living relationship with Him in contrast to "Christianity,"

> All who have become followers of Jesus have become one body; they have received one Spirit.

which they say is simply a religion, a cultural label, or a political category. There is value in doing this because it focuses attention on the main thing, the thing that all Christians share in common.

But when we contrast a relationship with Jesus and Christianity, we do not mean to say that the long history of Christianity has no value or that heroes from the past have nothing to teach us. In every age since Jesus, there have been Christian movements that shared living and saving faith in Jesus. While in some cases much of the spiritual fervor has been lost, the spiritual essence of these movements of God's Spirit remains, and many who follow Christ in a variety of church traditions do have living faith.

The missionary work of the church of Jesus Christ is a glorious story, full of heroes and martyrs. It is amazing that over two billion people, one-third of the earth's population, profess to be Christians, especially when we consider that Jesus gave his Great Commission to a small band of doubting disciples. This has come about through the heroic efforts of disciples of Jesus over 2,000 years of church history. These brothers and sisters may not have worshipped exactly as we do. Most lived before the video screen, and many even before the printing press! There have always been, and there remain today, differences in theology. Yet there are powerful and inspiring stories from every century of how disciples of Jesus Christ have spread the good news about salvation in Him. All of the history of the church belongs to every believer in Jesus.

Some think that the church of Jesus got nothing

accomplished between the death of the apostle John in AD 100 and the protest of Martin Luther in 1517, but such thinking robs us of our history. Time does not permit us to look at the whole story, but allow me to briefly mention moments in this story that are worth pursuing in greater depth as you have the time and interest.

The book of Acts tells about the westward movement of the church through the missionary journeys of the apostle Paul. Shortly after Paul reached Rome, Christians were reported in France and in Tunisia, North Africa. Thaddeus took the good news **All of the history of the church belongs to every believer in Jesus.** to Armenia, which became the first Christian nation and remains to this day a light in a predominantly Muslim region.[58]

But the church did not only move westward. By AD 100, the city of Arbela, present day Erbil in Iraq, had become a center of the Assyrian church in the East, which would take the message of Christ eastward through Central Asia, all the way to China. Before AD 200, Pantaenus of Alexandria had gone to India in response to an appeal for Christian teachers, missionaries had arrived in Japan, and Tertullian could write that Christianity had penetrated all ranks of society in North Africa.

It has been estimated that 10 percent of the world's population had become Christians by AD 300.

Before AD 400, Christianity had become the official faith of the Roman Empire, and Jerome would write,

"From India to Britain, all nations resound with the death and resurrection of Christ." The great evangelist of that era, John Chrysostom opened a school for native Gothic evangelists with these words: "*Go and make disciples of all nations* was not said for the apostles only, but for us also."

In the fifth century, Patrick went to Ireland, first as a slave of Irish pirates, then later, after his escape, as a missionary bringing the love of Christ to the land of his suffering.

In the sixth century, a man named Augustine and a team of missionaries were sent to England to reintroduce the gospel. The missionaries settled in Canterbury, and within a year had baptized 10,000 people.

In the seventh century, the first Christian missionaries to China, Nestorian monks from Asia Minor and Persia led by a monk named Alopen, arrived in the Middle Kingdom. In this same century, which saw the birth of Islam, the Bible was translated into Arabic for the first time.

In the eighth century, Boniface evangelized the pagan tribes of Germany, and early in the ninth century, the emperor Charlemagne championed the preaching of the good news in the languages of the European peoples – the Romance and Germanic languages – not just official church languages of Greek, Hebrew, and Latin.

The good news was established in Russia in the ninth century by two monks, Cyril and Methodius, and within a generation, virtually the entire population had heard the good news.

In the tenth century, the Hungarians, Danes, and

Poles received the good news, and the Swedes and Norwegians heard the gospel in the eleventh century. By the end of the twelfth century, the Bible was available in twenty-two different languages.

In the thirteenth century, Francis of Assisi heard a sermon on Matthew 10, in which Jesus sent out his disciples to preach, taking nothing with them, and he launched a movement to do just that! Among his early followers was Ramon Llull, who devoted his life to bringing the good news to Muslims. Others went with the good news to China, Sumatra, Java, and Borneo. In the same century, Dominic of Guzman started a new movement of preachers devoted to the salvation of souls in the growing cities in the languages of the peoples; his followers quickly traveled to Africa and Asia, to places where the church had not yet gone.

In the fourteenth century, the Dominican missionary explorer Jordanus Catalani took the good news to the diverse peoples of South Asia. He left an account of his travels, *Mirabilia*, that opened Asia to Europeans.

The conflict between Islam and Christianity began during the lifetime of Muhammad (who died in 632) and has flared periodically ever since. In one episode in 1389, large numbers of Christians marched through the streets of Cairo, denouncing Islam and lamenting that they had abandoned the religion of their fathers because of fear of persecution. They were beheaded, both men and women, and a fresh persecution of Christians followed.

Also in the fourteenth century, on a large island in the Atlantic Ocean, the Bible was translated into an obscure language called English, by a man named John Wycliff. When I'm explaining to people the reason we have translated the *JESUS* film, based on the Gospel of Luke, into more than 1,500 languages, I often jokingly remind them that Jesus didn't speak English. Someone translated the gospel into English for us – and he was declared a heretic for doing it!

All of this took place before the Protestant Reformation! But make no mistake about it, this history belongs to all believers! It belongs to us, to those who are seeking to take the good news to everyone, everywhere. And before you decide that the Christianity these heroes preached was in some way substandard, please take the time to read their stories. We sometimes make the mistake of thinking that nothing good happened in the history of missions until the sixteenth century, when Protestantism arose, or even the nineteenth century, when English speakers went to other nations! But such thinking robs us of the testimony of 1,500 years of passionate and heroic men and women who took the good news around the world.

At the same time, there is no question that the Reformers' emphasis on preaching the basics of justification by faith contributed to a new era of global missions. John Calvin sent French Huguenots to Brazil in the middle of the sixteenth century. Protestant scholars called attention to the Great Commission. Hadrian á Saravia, one of the translators of the King James Bible, wrote a book in which he made what was then the controversial argument that the Great Commission was binding on the present-day church since the apostles had not fulfilled it.

In the seventeenth century, Puritan scholar Richard Sibbes wrote that the good news must be preached "til it have gone over the whole world." Protestant churches were soon responding. The German Lutheran Church sent Peter Heyling to Ethiopia, and a young man named John Eliot devoted his life to reaching out to the Algonquin tribe in a place called Massachusetts. Quaker missionaries were soon dispatched to the New World, and the Anglican Society for the Propagation of the Gospel in Foreign Parts was formed for the "evangelization of the non-Christian races of the world."

The spirit of eighteenth-century Protestant missions was epitomized by Isaac Watts's great hymn "Jesus Shall Reign Where'er the Sun." Count Nicolaus Ludwig Zinzendorf and his Moravian church at Herrnhut began their rapidly expanding work among slaves in the Caribbean and the Inuit in Greenland. A "Great Awakening" among Protestants on both sides of the Atlantic gave rise to a call for "Concerts of Prayer" for all the people of the world. Thomas Coke, a leader of the Methodist movement, presented a "Plan of the Society for the Establishment of Missions Among the Heathen," and Baptist William Carey wrote his historic work, *An Enquiry into the Obligations of Christians to Use Means for the Conversion of the Heathens.* The first great era of Protestant missions was under way!

The nineteenth century would see a Second Great Awakening among Protestants, centered in America, with such legendary moments as the "haystack prayer meeting" at Williams College, the founding of the American Board of Commissioners for Foreign Missions, and the sending of its first missionary, Adoniram Judson. Also in this century were the founding of the American Bible Society and the sending of Baptist Lott Carey, the first African-American missionary. The mission movement would grow under innovative leaders such as Henry Venn, who articulated the principles of "self-governing, self-supporting, and self-propagating" indigenous churches, and Hudson Taylor (missionary to China), who broke new ground in indigenization. Missionary pioneers such as David Livingstone pushed deep into the continent of Africa. Tireless crusaders like Lottie Moon brought the role of women in global missions into focus. This was the heyday of the traditional American Protestant denominations, and Baptists, Presbyterians, Methodists, Disciples of Christ, and a dozen other denominational fellowships could each recite its litany of missionary heroes going to the remotest parts of the earth.

The Student Volunteer Movement kicked off the twentieth century, in which the American Protestant missionary effort would move to the forefront of global missions. John R. Mott explained the movement's mission statement in his book *The Evangelization of the World in This Generation* (1900): To give all people alive an adequate chance to know Jesus Christ as Savior and to become His real disciples. Mott argued that it was the personal obligation of every believer to participate in this task of making sure that the message is well understood in every language and every culture.

The work of the Protestant denominations was assisted by the adherents of several movements in American Christianity. The Fundamentalist and Pentecostal movements of the early century, and then the mid-century Neo-evangelical and the late-century Evangelical movement each added to the ranks of American missionaries. One key development was the formation of dozens of faith mission societies, created to build nondenominational coalitions, sometimes focused on one part of the world; among them were the China Inland Mission (now OMF International), the Sudan Interior Mission (SIM), the African Inland Mission (AIM), and The Evangelical Alliance Mission (TEAM). Despite the suffering and disillusionment of two world wars and the theological wrangling centered on liberal theology and the social gospel emphasis, the effort continued to accelerate.

By mid-century, the effort was served by a variety of specialized ministries, such as Bible translation agencies like Wycliffe Bible Translators, logistical support agencies like Mission Aviation Fellowship, and the many Christian broadcasters previously mentioned. University students were once again in the forefront, with thousands responding to Inter-Varsity's missionary conventions and Bill Bright's call to "come help change the world."

By the late-twentieth century, a comprehensive strategy to evangelize the world was being discussed at global meetings like the Lausanne Congress of World Evangelization. Several denominational mission boards, most notably the Southern Baptists and the Assemblies of God, were hitting their full stride. New movements of young people like Youth with a Mission were bringing fresh energy and innovation to the mission. The U.S. Center for World Mission was talking about reaching the remaining unreached people groups, and the Jesus Film Project was working to give everyone, everywhere the chance to see and hear Jesus speaking to them in their own heart language. A powerful church was emerging in the countries that were previously considered "Third World," developing, or less developed. These countries comprised the Global South that arose to take its place in world missions.[59]

The growth of the Catholic Church since the Reformation has also been significant. The Catholic Church is a diverse church – every bit as diverse as Protestantism. And while some Protestants may lament that the evangelistic preaching of the good news has not always been clearly in focus, the religious orders of the Catholic Church enabled the rapid expansion of Christian teaching into the Americas, Asia, and Africa.

One cannot read the accounts of the heroic work of Francis Xavier, Matteo Ricci, Roberto de Nobili, and others throughout Asia, the tragic history of the "reductions" of South America (which was depicted in the movie *The Mission* and which led to the suppression of the Jesuit order for a quarter century), or the story of Jean de Brebeuf and the hundreds of martyrs in North America without feeling the spiritual kinship among all who seek to take the good news to the whole world.

We must also value the contributions to global missions made by the Orthodox branch of the church. The branches of the historic church that have remained distinct from the Roman Catholic Church since the eleventh century include the churches of Russia, Eastern Europe, Greece, Ethiopia, Armenia, and large numbers of believers throughout the Middle East and India. Although the work of the largest Orthodox churches has been marked with suffering during their long struggle with Islamic empires and a seventy-year battle with Marxist Communism, Orthodox Christians nevertheless made up over 10 percent of the Christian family as of the year 2000.

We followers of Jesus Christ share one history. We are involved in one mission. We must also remember that simply taking to oneself the name of Jesus Christ – regardless of what one's devotional practice may be – is in itself a radical step. **Just taking the name of Jesus can get you killed.** In much of the world, there is nothing to be gained (in this life) by claiming to be a Christian. In fact, confessing Christ can be dangerous, regardless of the church one attends – or fails to attend. Those who are chopping off the heads of Christians in the Middle East, for example, do not stop to ask whether the believer is Catholic, Protestant, or Orthodox, or how faithful a follower he or she is. Just taking the name of Jesus can get you killed.

We suffer together as Christians. Can we work together as Christians? Can we see this story of the church of Jesus Christ fulfilling its mission as one story? Can we rejoice together in what we have accomplished? Can we support one another in making sure that every professing Christian has a personal relationship with Jesus Christ and is mobilized to share his or her faith with others? Can we work together on evangelization as one church without fighting about the nonessential matters that divide us? Can we eliminate duplication and competition and go forward in one united effort to give everyone, everywhere a chance to know Jesus?

There are many promising signs.

One is the unprecedented degree of unity evident among Christians who are working to identify and make meaningful contact with the people groups in the world who have not yet been engaged with the good news of Jesus. In the year 2000, Billy Graham convened a conference in Amsterdam for more than ten thousand evangelists from around the world. One part of the conference involved a gathering of six hundred mission leaders focused around the topic of completing the Great Commission. At that gathering, Paul Eshleman, founder of the Jesus Film Project, explained the biblical concept of "people group," the basic unit of people who share a single language and culture. He made the case for identifying and targeting all of the people groups with populations of ten thousand or more in the world that had no exposure to the message of Jesus (at that time they numbered around 230). Bruce Wilkinson, the emcee for the meeting, came to the podium and said, "There shouldn't be any unengaged people groups in the world. We aren't doing our job; let's finish it!" He challenged the organizations present to look at the list of unengaged groups, take ownership of some of them, and come forward to make that commitment. God moved on the group, and the atmosphere was electric as people came forward, many of them weeping, to take responsibility for unengaged groups.

Suddenly everything stopped. One hundred and forty-one of the groups had been claimed, and no one else was coming forward. The hall went quiet. Back at Table 71, Steve Douglass, President of Cru, leaned over to Mark Anderson of YWAM and said, "Why don't our two organizations take the rest?" This set off a buzz of conversation around the table as leaders from Wycliffe Bible Translators, the Southern Baptist International Mission Board, and other key groups joined in agreement. Then somebody came up with a note that said simply, "Table 71 takes the rest!"[60]

This event set off a series of cooperative meetings that have continued for the last sixteen years and have become a growing coalition of evangelical organizations committed to engaging every people group with the good news of Jesus. Members of the coalition say that they have experienced unprecedented interagency cooperation since making the pledge to work together toward this common goal, and several additional cooperative structures, including the Issachar Initiative and Finishing the Task have resulted, promoting the idea of eliminating duplication and competition among evangelical groups.

This fresh movement builds on the work of mission collaboration built by strategists like Phil Butler, who founded Interdev in the 1980s to coordinate the work of ministries working in "gateway people groups." By 2002, Interdev had assisted in the formation of ninety-two regional partnerships involving more than three thousand organizations. Today, its successor organization, visionSynergy, continues to build multilateral, multinational partnerships of Christian workers in key areas of the world.[61]

Another encouraging development is the large number of those within the existing historic church traditions who are working to make sure that everyone in their churches is evangelized. Many members within the Catholic and Orthodox traditions are working to make sure that every professing Christian in their churches has a personal relationship with Jesus. They are encouraged by leaders like Pope Francis, who wrote in his *The Joy of the Gospel*:

> The primary reason for evangelizing is the love of Jesus which we have received, the experience of salvation which urges us to ever greater love of him. What kind of love would not feel the need to speak of the beloved, to point him out, to make him known? If we do not feel an intense desire to share this love, we need to pray insistently that he will once more touch our hearts. We need to implore his grace daily, asking him to open our cold hearts and shake up our lukewarm and superficial existence.[62]

Many of us Westerners grew up with lukewarm and superficial Christianity, where there was no evidence of the love of Jesus or the experience of salvation, and so we rejected Christianity as practiced by our churches.

I attended such a church throughout my childhood without ever hearing the good news clearly presented. When I was finally evangelized at high school, I was angry at the church of my youth. I quickly joined a Jesus Movement church made up of passionate believers. We were very sure that we all understood all of God's truth very well, and we acted as if it were all equally important.

Based on my own experience, I rejected the idea that one could have living faith and be part of a church in which not everyone shared that faith. The idea that a true follower of Jesus could stay in such a church – especially if it disagreed with mine on nonessential matters – was very difficult for me to accept.

It was Richard Lovelace, emeritus professor of church history at Gordon-Conwell Theological Seminary, who greatly helped me when I was a young opinionated pastor to be open to God's grace working in places that I least expected it. He pointed out that God had worked in Christian groups that disagreed with one another on many points and that "genuine experience of Christ" was the important matter.[63]

God has done great things in and through Christians in many traditions, and He continues to do great things! Movements of believers actively sharing their faith are found in all kinds of places, both within and outside the traditional church. It is more important to work together to reach those who do not know Jesus than to fight with fellow believers over secondary matters.

Let us cooperate as much as we can in proclaiming the good news of Jesus to everyone, everywhere.

Chapter 9

From Everywhere to Everywhere

When Jesus gave the Great Commission to His disciples, He told them to take the gospel from Jerusalem to Judea and Samaria and even to the "ends of the earth." Of course "the ends of the earth" is a figure of speech meaning "everywhere," but I wonder, as they stood there in what we now call the Middle East, what the disciples thought of as "the ends of the earth." If they had understood the world as we do today, they may have realized that Jerusalem is at 31°47'08" N, 35°12'52"E. If you go 180 degrees around the globe and same latitude south of the equator, you get to the point 3147'08" S, 144°47'08" W, which (according to Google Earth) is a point in the South Pacific that is not really near much of anything. The water is about seventeen thousand feet deep there. But of course, the disciples would not have known that much geography.

Perhaps they considered Jesus' words in terms of the ancient cultures of the Bible as they knew it – the Law and the Prophets. If so, perhaps they thought of Egypt, Mesopotamia, and Persia as the ends of the earth. Maybe their context was the Greco-Roman world of their day – the lands conquered by the Roman Empire. If so, maybe they thought of the lands of Central Asia, North Africa, and strange tribes of Germania and Britannia as "the ends of the earth." I wonder if they thought of the ancient civilizations of India and China and North America, or if they even knew of them.

In God's providence, the gospel traveled west, where it took root at the center of the Roman Empire. It traveled east as well, but the church of the East was destined to be a suffering church. Through twenty centuries of persecution, the church survived in the East, but seldom flourished. So Christianity became known as a Western religion, despite the fact that it is the most widely dispersed of all the world's major religions. Christianity shaped the culture of the West in significant ways, and it continues to do so.

Christianity is no longer a Western religion!

But let's bring the story up to date.

Christianity is no longer a Western religion!

In 2013, Campus Crusade for Christ International did a survey asking, "Do you know someone who truly follows Jesus?" Here are the percentages of people who answered yes to that question by continent:

Africa......................... 59%

South America 54%

Asia 53%

North America........ 46%

Australia 42%

Europe...................... 29%[64]

Africans, South Americans, and Asians are more likely to know a true follower of Jesus than people from what we have known as the *Christian* West!

One of the first to call this to our attention was Philip Jenkins, a professor of history at Penn State. In his books *The Next Christendom* (2002) and *The New Faces of Christianity* (2008), he pointed out that 60 percent of the estimated two billion Christians in the world live in Africa, Asia, or Latin America. Jenkins estimated that by 2050 there would be an estimated three billion Christians, 75 percent of whom would live in what is called the "Global South."[65] Researchers at the Center for the Study of Global Christianity and Operation World confirm that the changes Jenkins described are taking place as he predicted. Today, 78 percent of the evangelical Christians in the world live in Africa, Asia, or Latin America![66]

God has done many amazing things within my generation's lifetime to bring this about.

Many areas of the world have especially exciting stories. Let's look at a few of them.

Korea

In 1886, Protestant missionaries baptized their very first

Korean convert. Korea was a Buddhist and Shamanist Asian nation. Today roughly one-third of South Koreans are Christians, and South Korea is home to ten of the eleven largest congregations in the world, including the Yoido Full Gospel Church in Seoul.[67] How did this happen?

The incredible growth of Korean Christianity actually began in North Korea and accelerated in a Pentecost-like outpouring of the Spirit of God in Pyongyang in 1907. Members of the still young First Church of Pyongyang heard about a revival going on in Wales, and soon more than one thousand members were gathered for a Bible study conference. As the story is told, "[Pastor] Lee asked two or three people to open [with prayer]. Twelve to twenty people started to lead. He said, 'If that's the way you want to lead, then let's all pray together out loud.' And that's when the wave rolled in." Another witness wrote, "The effect was indescribable – not of confusion, but a vast harmony of sound and spirit, a mingling together of souls moved by an irresistible impulse of prayer. The prayer sounded to me like the falling of many waters, an ocean of prayer beating against God's throne. It was not many, but one, born of one Spirit, lifted to one Father above." When the service ended, more than one-third of the congregation stayed, many crying out to God as if in pain.[68]

For those around the world who have experienced "Korean-style" prayer, that's where it got its start!

But the growth of Korean Christianity cannot be explained by one revival meeting alone. In addition to faithful preaching of the Word, fervent prayer, compassionate lifestyle, and perseverance in suffering, two factors are worth noting. First, Korean Christianity has been a genuine "people movement," spread by the bold witness of every believer, not just the leaders. The good news spread through families and networks of relationships in Korea because every new believer was an outspoken witness to her or his new faith. Second, Korea took the message of Christ as its own. Aided by the distribution of heart-language Scripture, self-sustaining funding, and national leadership, Koreans affirmed that the God of the Book is the God of Koreans. Christianity came to be seen as the true faith of the Korean people; Confucianism, Shintoism, and Communism were all seen as alien imports that threatened to take the people from true faith.[69]

Although North Korea is suffering under a brutal anti-Christian regime, South Koreans have never stopped praying and believing that it will one day be set free and reclaim its title of the Jerusalem of the East.[70]

Koreans also affirm that the God of the Book is the God of all nations. The 2012 Korean World Mission Conference celebrated the sending of the twenty-thousandth Korean missionary, and the presence of Korean missionaries in 169 countries![71] Although the United States sends more total cross-cultural missionaries than South Korea, by another measure South Korea sends far more: the USA sends 614 missionaries for every million church members, while South Korea sends 1,014![72]

A tragic story that few Westerners know contributed to my own appreciation for the effectiveness of Korean missionaries. In 1937, Stalin brutally packed 170,000 Koreans into cattle cars and deported them to the steppe country of Central Asia, irrationally fearing that they might be Japanese agents. About 40,000 died of starvation and exposure over the next two years. Those who survived found themselves in the Soviet republics of Kazakhstan and Uzbekistan, where they attempted to adjust to the traditional Muslim, Turko-Persian culture. Many lived the harsh life of the Soviet collective farm and then endured the increased suffering during the total collapse of the Soviet system.

As Koreans responded to God's call to the world, they remembered their fellow Koreans in Central Asia. Dozens of brave missionary families moved to these countries in the 1990s to bring the good news to their Korean families who had been practically cut off from Christian contact for two generations. As many former Soviet Koreans responded to the message brought to them from Korea, they joined their fellow Koreans in taking the message beyond their own people group to the Kazakh, Uzbek, Tajik, Karakalpak, and other peoples of the region.[73]

We had the privilege of working alongside a brave team of Korean missionaries for several years. Their style seemed intense to many of us Americans; they insisted on living in community with their local disciples and spending long hours in prayer and study. But the fruit of their lives was undeniable, and the times of prayer we spent with them are some of most powerful we have ever experienced.

Sub-Saharan Africa

Another area of the world that is experiencing incredible church growth is the part of Africa south of the Saharan desert. From 1910 to 2010, the Christian population in the fifty-one countries of Sub-Saharan Africa grew from 9 percent to 63 percent.[74] Around five hundred million Christians, one-fifth of all the Christians in the world, live in this area.[75] This region contains many of the countries with the largest Christian populations in the world, including Nigeria, the Democratic Republic of Congo, Ethiopia, South Africa, Kenya, and Uganda.[76] Moreover, the total population in Sub-Saharan Africa is expected to grow at a faster pace than in any other region in the decades ahead, and more than double by 2050. This would bring the number of Christians to nearly one billion![77] If it is already incorrect today to think of Christianity as a Western religion, what might be the reality by 2050!

This amazing Christian movement may actually represent the most dramatic advance of the Christian faith in all of human history. The movement began with the planting of the good news by Western missionaries in the eighteenth and nineteenth centuries, but it has had to fight through the accompanying evils of racism, slavery, and spiritual imperialism. The growth of African Christianity has been accelerated by African leaders, particularly Pentecostals, who have shaped and molded it to fit the African context.[78] It is no wonder that the missionaries who witnessed this miraculous growth agree with Andrew Walls, a former missionary in West Africa and Professor Emeritus of the Study of Christianity in the Non-Western World at the University of Edinburgh, who has called the twentieth century "the most remarkable of the Christian centuries since the first."[79]

Bekele Shanko, Vice President of Global Church Movements for Campus Crusade for Christ International, is a product of this amazing faith-filled atmosphere of Sub-Saharan Christianity. He was born in a rural village in Ethiopia. His father was a Satan worshipper and alcoholic who had demonic power. His father was able to bring rain and stop rain; when he cursed people, they died. Demons ran his family. They told the father to get up at 5:00 a.m. and begin to drink alcohol from a big glass and smoke continuously; they forced him to beat his three wives every day. The family was not allowed to eat before offering some food to the demon who lived behind the house under a big coffee tree. Whenever Bekele's father failed to obey the demons, they would punish the family. Immediately, a child would die; twelve children died in this way. Bekele was not given a name by his parents until he was four years old because they didn't know if he would live or die. When he made it to four, they named him Bekele, which means "he has become, he has grown." When Bekele was five, demons told his father to dedicate Bekele to serve Satan. He began to drink and smoke and became the disciple of his father.

Later that year, God sent two angels to visit Bekele's

father. They took him to heaven and hell and asked which he would choose. He said he would choose heaven. The angels said they would send two men to him to tell him how he could get into heaven. That was on a Wednesday. On Friday, two young Christians came to Bekele's father saying that God had prompted them to come to tell him how to accept Jesus and deny demons. Bekele and his father both believed in Jesus on that day.

On Sunday of that week, Bekele's father was walking with his cows by the river and found a New Testament on the ground. He heard a voice saying, "This is my word." He answered, "God, I can't read. Will you help me to read it?" Immediately, he was able to read the Bible. That afternoon he called the whole village to his place; all four hundred people came, fearing the power he had possessed. He told his story about the angels, the two men, and the Book. He read 1 John 5:11-13: *And this is the testimony: God has given us eternal life, and this life is in his Son. Whoever has the Son has life; whoever does not have the Son of God does not have life. I write these things to you who believe in the name of the Son of God so that you may know that you have eternal life.* All four hundred people asked Jesus to come into their lives that night. For thirty-seven years, until his death in 2013, Bekele's father could read only the Bible. When Bekele asked him how that could be when the letters are the same in other books, he replied, "When I open the Bible, a great light shines on the book and my eyes can see."

Bekele went away to college, then got a prestigious job working for the government. He was given a full scholarship to study in the USA, but four weeks into his time in the USA, God spoke to him and challenged him to return to Ethiopia to serve Him. He returned and joined the staff of Campus Crusade for Christ. In 1998, living in Addis Ababa, he launched a project to mobilize the churches to reach the city in fifty-two days, as Nehemiah rebuilt the walls of his city in fifty-two days. The project succeeded in training ten thousand believers to share their faith in a variety of ways, and forty-nine thousand people came to know Christ in fifty-two days. Later, Bekele became the Campus Crusade area leader for Southern and Eastern Africa and moved to Zimbabwe. He sensed God telling him He would do fifty times more than he had done in Addis Ababa. Bekele launched a project to evangelize fifty cities (in twenty-three nations) in fifty days. He and his team shared the vision, trained five hundred thousand volunteers from twenty thousand churches and three hundred mission organizations, and shared the good news of Jesus with 64.5 million people in fifty days; 1,720,000 people indicated decisions to become followers of Jesus – in fifty days.[80]

His experiences in Africa convinced Bekele of the power in unity. He says, "Churches are ready to work together; they are waiting for a vision to unite them." Today he leads the Global Alliance for Church Multiplication (GACX), which unites the efforts of more than sixty groups to finish the challenge of telling everyone, everywhere about Jesus.[81]

Global leadership is coming from the African church. One expression of this is the way that Sub-Saharan

Christians are owning the task of evangelizing their own continent – specifically the Muslim north. One movement is called "Go North," and it is envisioning and mobilizing believers to share their faith in countries and areas where Westerners can scarcely go.

One Christian leader mobilized a group of college student disciples to go north into an area that had not had a Christian presence in a thousand years. Word spread that they were in the market sharing the good news with people, and antagonistic religious leaders challenged them, saying that if Jesus had power He should heal a certain demon-possessed man in the village. The students took a bold step of faith and asked to see the man. They prayed over him through the night while reading Scripture, worshipping the Lord, and commanding the demons to come out of him. By morning, God had delivered him.

The man proclaimed to everyone in the town that Jesus healed him. Enraged by this turn of events, the religious leaders beat the students and drove them out of town. Undaunted, the students returned, this time going directly to the town market where they distributed hundreds of *JESUS* film DVDs. Once again, the religious leaders ordered them beaten, and then they were arrested. They spent that night in jail where they encountered six suspected members of an international terrorist group. The Holy Spirit continued working through the boldness of these students. By night's end, all six suspected terrorists, along with a police officer who heard their testimony during the night, were transformed by the power of the good news and received Christ as their Savior. An underground church was born – where there had not been a single known Christian for a thousand years – made up of a police officer who had beaten these college students, a man delivered from demons, six former terrorists, and their families.

Three years later, the ministry director who had sent the students visited this underground church. He reported that it was flourishing, having grown to forty members. They were active in distributing copies of the *JESUS* film and were talking about planting another church![82]

The boldness of African Christians is remarkable. There were more than 1.8 million people killed for their faith in Christ in Africa in the twentieth century, and yet the church perseveres.

Latin America

For several centuries, more than 90 percent of Latin Americans have been professing Catholics; however, Latin Americans often mixed spiritist religious practices and the traditional myths of native peoples into the Christian life in questionable ways. Much has gone on within and without the Catholic Church in recent decades to clarify the gospel for Latin Americans and to purify and renew their practice of the Christian life. Within the Catholic Church, the Charismatic Renewal movement has swept the church and led to a focus on the work of the Holy Spirit and personal faith in Christ. A large portion of the Catholic Church in every Latin American country identifies itself as charismatic, including over half the Catholics in Brazil, Panama, Honduras, the Dominican Republic, and El Salvador. Other Latin American Catholics have gained a fresh appreciation for personal Bible reading through the practice of Lectio Divina, a method of reading and meditating on Scripture.

At the same time, many Latin Americans are responding to the message of Protestants, particularly Pentecostal movements and charismatic forms of traditional evangelical denominations.

The church of Jesus Christ is flourishing in Latin America.

The church of Jesus Christ is flourishing in Latin America. In both Catholic and Protestant settings, there are Christians who are focusing on personal faith, the power of the Holy Spirit, engaging with Scripture through prayer and meditation, and proclaiming the good news.[83]

Brazil is the most striking example of the rapid changes taking place in Latin American Christianity. Brazil is home to more Catholics than any other country in the world – over 120 million. At the same time, Brazilians are leaving the Catholic Church to become Protestants at a rapid rate. According to one recent study, over half of Brazilians, more than 100 million people, will be evangelical Christians by 2020. The rapid growth of evangelicalism in Brazil has been publicly credited with a decline in alcoholism, an increase in school enrollment, and a reduction in failed marriages.[84]

Brazilian churches are increasing their missionary force. "Brazilians are accepted in many countries around the world where Americans would never be accepted," says Alan Mullins, who has been a missionary in Brazil for thirty years. "There are churches supporting up to fifteen missionaries, many of them in Europe, some here working with Indians. There is a real move for missions in Brazil that I've not seen in my thirty years here."[85]

China

More followers of Jesus will worship this Sunday in China than in the United States. The incredible story of Christian growth in China begins with the end of the Cultural Revolution in 1976. The brutal ten-year persecution of Christians quickly turned to a new opportunity for the spread of the Christian faith.

Former US president Jimmy Carter tells the story of a significant moment in this process. Then Vice Premier Minister of China, Deng Xiaoping, who later became China's Premier Minister, was visiting the White House in 1979. "In a very private moment," Carter recounts, "he and I talked about faith, what he believed, and what I believed. I liked to chat with many Communist leaders about their faith." Deng Xiaoping asked President Carter for suggestions about Christianity in China. Carter shared three. First, Carter suggested that Chinese Christians should have Bibles, and knowing how strongly China wished to be free of foreign interference, he reminded Deng Xiaoping that if China did not print Bibles, foreigners would smuggle them in. Mr. Deng Xiaoping replied, "We will print Bibles in China."

As we now know, Deng Xiaoping gave the order, not only to print Bibles, but to use Bible paper which had been imported for printing Mao Zedong's *Collected Works*, and to print a large quantity of Bibles on a military printing press in Nanjing, China. Soon after, the United Bible Society and the Three-Self Patriotic Movement/China Christian Council (TSPM/CCC) worked together to create Amity Press in Nanjing, which had printed more than 150 million Bibles in China as of June 2016!

Carter continued. "Religious freedom is in the constitution of China." Carter's second suggestion was that China needed to reopen churches. People who believe in God need a place to worship. Deng Xiaoping answered, "We will reopen the churches in China."

At the time of the conversation between Deng and Carter, Xiaoling Zhu, Executive for East Asia and Pacific for the United Church of Christ, was a young boy in China. "I remembered that my father, an ordained pastor, received a notice from upper level government to go to the local government for the key to the church, which was owned by the local government and used as a meeting hall. I accompanied my father to ask for the key. I vividly saw the city mayor release the key, and my father opened the church. We worshipped God the next Sunday." The people of God have gathered there every Sunday since.

Thirdly, since Christian missions have no country boundaries, Carter suggested that China should let missionaries in. Deng Xiaoping was quiet for a while and then said, "I will give you an answer tomorrow morning." The next day, Deng Xiaoping stated to Jimmy Carter, "No." Outside missionary activity is still forbidden in China, but in fairness, it is easy to understand the Chinese position. During the Opium Wars (1840-1848), Western missionaries were used by their countries, because of their language skills, to write many unequal treaties between the Qing Dynasty and Western countries. These treaties demanded that China open trade and open churches. There was an unholy alliance between the church and the military arm of the Western states.[86]

Christianity has flourished in China in the last thirty-five years. Official estimates say that there are twenty-three million members of the official Protestant churches of the TSPM/CCC and five million Catholics. But this is only the tip of the iceberg: there are as many as 140 million Christians in unregistered house churches meeting all across China. House churches come in many forms and sizes. They include hidden meetings in rural homes, gatherings in factories, small Bible study groups started by students, and semi-public gatherings of over one thousand. The massive participation of young people has led some to estimate that China will be home to 250 million Christians by 2030.[87]

Chinese Christians are also owning the task of sharing the good news with the minority peoples within their borders. There are fifty-six recognized minority groups within China, making up nearly 10 percent of its population. One team recently reported that they were sharing the good news of Jesus with a Buddhist monk who was considered by his followers to be a "Living Buddha." After many conversations and viewings of the *JESUS* film, this monk has become a follower of Jesus and is leading his own followers into this new relationship with God!

China has also become a mission-sending country. Thousands have taken up the call, "Back to Jerusalem." Three leaders of the house-church movement, Brother Yun, Peter Xu Yongze, and Enoch Wang, who collectively have spent more than forty years in prison for their faith, have laid out the vision to send at least one hundred thousand missionaries back along the Silk Road through Muslim lands, back to Jerusalem – taking the good news of Jesus Christ to people who could never be reached by Westerners. I have personally had the privilege of being in training sessions with the first of these recruits, and can testify to their quality and their commitment to this great vision.[88]

> China has also become a mission-sending country.

Albert W. Hickman, Senior Research Associate at the Center for the Study of Global Christianity, Gordon-Conwell Theological Seminary (CSGC), sums up very well what we have seen in this chapter: "In the past, missions was largely 'from the West to the Rest.' Today the number of international missionaries from the Global South continues to increase, even as the number of missionaries sent from the Global North is decreasing. South Korea has been joined by Brazil and Nigeria as major missionary-sending countries, and others are poised to follow."[89]

In its latest study, the CSGC reported:

- Christians sent out approximately 400,000 international missionaries in 2010.

- The United States still tops the chart by far in terms of total missionaries.

- Of the ten countries sending the most missionaries in 2010, three were in the Global South: Brazil, South Korea, and India.

- Other notable missionary senders included South Africa, the Philippines, Mexico, China, Colombia, and Nigeria.

My conclusion is simply this: Although the USA and other Western countries still have a crucial role to play in completing Christ's Great Commission, the Christian mission is now from everyone to everywhere.[90]

In most cases, the best people to reach unreached villages, towns, and neighborhoods are people from nearby. Often a strong church has members whose first language is the predominant language of a nearby group; often they have relatives or friends who live nearby.

This principle is illustrated well in a Cambodian village that I had the privilege of visiting. The leader, Phean, and his wife first heard the good news through the *JESUS* film in 2006, brought by a team of Westerners. Phean thought, "What kind of saving power is that brought by these big white people?" Nonetheless, Phean recognized his need to be transformed by God and became a follower of Jesus. Next, Phean and the other new believers began to meet as a house church and were trained on how to share their faith with others and encouraged to pray about whom to share with. Phean thought right away of a friend, Daravuth, who was the principal of a nearby school. Daravuth came to faith and also started a house church. Daravuth was a well-known person, and his church soon grew to sixteen churches. Now Phean and Daravuth share the vision of seeing a house church in every village in their province and are well on the way to this goal.[91]

This Cambodia movement illustrates a four-step process: (1) Someone comes from "the outside" to an unengaged area to bring the good news; (2) The new local believers are trained to share their faith; (3) The movement multiplies as local believers take leadership and ownership; (4) The vision and plan for reaching a whole area comes into being.

Everyone will have a chance to know Jesus, as local believers around the world go to the next village, the next neighborhood, the next high-rise apartment, and the next digital community with the good news.

Chapter 10

Jesus Followers Everywhere

My vision is to see movements everywhere, so that everyone knows someone who truly follows Jesus.[92] A movement is a groundswell of committed followers of Jesus who pray and work together, believing God for an impact that only the Holy Spirit can deliver.[93]

I have had the privilege of being a part of the Jesus Movement of the 1970s. I have also studied movements like the two Great Awakenings in America and Europe, the Welsh revival that spread around the world as far as Korea in the early twentieth century, and church renewal movements that brought new life to members of historic churches in the late-twentieth century. Never has there been the possibility of inter-related global movements of Jesus followers like we see beginning to happen today. I am convinced that we live in the most exciting moment in the history of the church.

Every great Jesus movement has these three factors:

(1) it is a work of the Holy Spirit; (2) it is an answer to fervent prayer; (3) it requires a unifying plan.

Only God, the Holy Spirit, can complete the job of sharing the good news of Jesus with everyone in the world. He empowers His people to love and to speak. He sets up divine encounters and arranges circumstances. He transforms hearts and changes behavior. He convicts sinners, He sanctifies saints, and He strengthens doubters. He encourages the down-hearted. He emboldens the timid. He comforts the persecuted. He heals the sick, He drives out demons, and He raises the dead!

We live in the age of the Holy Spirit. It began on the day of Pentecost, as the apostle Peter announced:

In the last days, God says,
I will pour out my Spirit on all people.
Your sons and daughters will prophesy,
your young men will see visions,
your old men will dream dreams.
Even on my servants, both men and women,
I will pour out my Spirit in those days,
and they will prophesy.
I will show wonders in the heavens above
and signs on the earth below,
blood and fire and billows of smoke.
The sun will be turned to darkness
and the moon to blood
before the coming of the great and glori-
ous day of the Lord.
And everyone who calls
on the name of the Lord will be saved.
(Acts 2:17-21)

There is a return to this first-century focus on the Holy Spirit in our day. Pentecostalism is by far the fastest growing segment within Protestantism. The Charismatic Renewal is a major force in Catholicism. Christians that would not see themselves as part of these groups nonetheless emphasize the role of the Holy Spirit in empowering the believer, making the believer holy and producing spiritual fruit in the believer's life.

The church is also experiencing a renewed emphasis on fervent prayer. Of course, many Catholic religious orders have emphasized prayer for generations. But these days, the church at large is beginning to pray more. The beautiful emphasis within Christian music on praise and adoration sung directly to God, with a special awareness of His presence, is remaking what many of us think of as worship. Prayer movements like that in South Korea, the Day of Prayer Movement out of South Africa, the International House of Prayer movement that began in Kansas City, 24/7 prayer chains, and the increased practice of fasting are but a few of the many evidences of a global prayer renewal.

> The church is also experiencing a renewed emphasis on fervent prayer.

Jesus asked his disciples regarding the temple, *Is it not written, 'My house shall be called a house of prayer for all the nations'?* (Mark 11:17 ESV). Today, the church is that house dedicated to praying for all nations.

Ask me, and I will make the nations your inheritance, the ends of the earth your possession, the Father says to the Son in Psalm 2:8. Today, we are joining Jesus in this prayer.

Prayer guides like that of Operation World and the Joshua Project are of great help to those of us who want to expand the horizons of our prayer.[94]

The work of the Holy Spirit in answer to fervent prayer is essential to spiritual movements, but there is also an element of human action; otherwise Jesus would not have said, "Go!" He might have said, "Stay here and pray; I've got this." But He sent us instead!

There is a famous African proverb that says, "If you want to go fast, go alone; if you want to go far, go together." To that I would add, "If you want to go fast and far, have a plan." Common action requires a clear plan and rich communication around the plan. A growing number of Great Commission groups are coming together around a plan to give everyone, everywhere a chance to know Jesus.

The plan involves two simple elements: multiplication and cooperation.

Multiplication means that every follower of Jesus is involved in reproducing themselves through evangelism and discipleship. It is based on the biblical principle expressed in 2 Timothy 2:2: *The things you have heard me say in the presence of many witnesses entrust to reliable people who will also be qualified to teach others.* There are four generations of disciples represented in this verse: (1) Paul, (2) Timothy, (3) reliable people, and (4) others.

Multiplication is a much more effective way of spreading a message than addition. It involves everyone, not just a single leader. It uses simple training to prepare every new follower to spread the good news and make disciples as part of her or his lifestyle.

Christian movements can spread very rapidly using this method. David Watson, a former missionary to India, saw forty thousand churches (averaging sixty-three members) started in fifteen years using simple principles of multiplication, prayer, and obedience-based Bible study. Watson defines churches as "groups of baptized believers in the Lord and Savior Jesus Christ that gather to worship, fellowship and nurture one another, and, outside of gatherings, endeavor to obey all the commands of Christ in order to transform families and communities." No building or paid ministers are necessary. Watson now acts as trainer and strategist for a network of two hundred thousand churches using his principles to foster "Church Planting Movements."[95]

These kinds of rapidly multiplying house churches are especially appropriate for some areas of the world, but what about areas of the world where historic churches already exist? They need renewal movements. One especially successful church renewal movement is based on the Alpha course, an eleven-week series of sessions built around discussions of talks or videos on basic Christianity hosted in a hospitable atmosphere. Alpha was born at Holy Trinity, Brompton, a Church of England parish in London, and is now used in every major denomination.[96]

The vision of the church everywhere is not new. The Discipling a Whole Nation (DAWN) movement, founded in 1984 by Jim Montgomery, worked from the premise that it would take the whole Body of Christ working together to reach each nation with the good news. They sought to mobilize all Christians to work together with the goal of "providing the incarnate presence of Christ in the form of local gatherings of believers within easy access of every person of every class, kind and condition." This idea was sometimes referred to as Saturation Church Planting (SCP) and was realized to some extent in over 150 countries, with a total of just over a million new churches started in the 1990s.[97]

The Global Alliance for Church Multiplication (GACX), a coalition of over forty church planting organizations, shares the vision of planting five million new churches and faith communities by 2020, so there will be a church for every thousand people who do not yet know Jesus – five million churches for five billion people. A church or faith community for every village, neighborhood high-rise apartment building, and digital community. The alliance has already seen nearly one million churches planted by member organizations since 2010.[98]

The Jesus Film Project, with our extensive network of partners, is in a unique position to see how God is at work among Protestants, Catholics, and Orthodox – historic churches and new church movements. Everybody uses the *JESUS* film – it is basically the Gospel of Luke on film, so everybody uses it. We have given ourselves to the vision of equipping every part of the Body of Christ with the tools they need to cooperate with every other part of the Body of Christ to reach everyone, everywhere with the good news of Jesus.

I recently made a trip to the Mara region of Tanzania where a wonderful partnership between Bible translators, church planting trainers, and nine very diverse denominations has resulted in the planting of many new churches in villages where none existed before. The partners laid aside their egos and their logos; no one is asking who should get the credit. They are all rejoicing that people who have never before heard the good news now have a living community of loving Jesus followers right in their midst!

Our team heard the testimony of a man, the father of eight, who watched the *JESUS* film produced by these partners and took it to his family. The family had been snake worshippers. A large snake regularly visited their mud-floored home and would "dance" as they threw meal to it. They had come to associate the presence of this snake with the well-being of their family. After watching the *JESUS* film together, the family decided to become followers of Jesus. Soon after, the snake returned to their home, but now it was hostile. At the same time, members of the family became sick and other bad things happened to them. They faced a decision: appease the snake or trust in Jesus. They chose Jesus and killed the snake. The man stood before us beaming with the news that all the members of his family were now well and that they felt incredible freedom!

We see it! It's within reach! God's people, working as partners. Movements everywhere, until everyone knows someone who truly follows Jesus!

Chapter 11

The Call to Everyone, Everywhere

Today, the church of Jesus Christ is returning again to the Great Commission: *All authority in heaven and on earth has been given to me. Therefore go and make disciples of all nations, baptizing them in the name of the Father and of the Son and of the Holy Spirit, and teaching them to obey everything I have commanded you. And surely I am with you always, to the very end of the age* (Matthew 28:18-20).

My ministry team was recently introduced to the concept of the "Founder's Mentality." Leading business analysts use this concept to identify the intense, insurgent sense of purpose that companies have when they are founded. Companies start out with a clear, compelling vision and a high sense of personal responsibility to see the vision implemented. Their founders are on the frontlines of the enterprise, putting everything on the line, doing the dirty work that leads to success. Then, in order to grow, businesses put processes and policies in place in order to achieve scale and scope. While much is gained in terms of systems and capacities, something essential can be lost. The enterprise can come to rely more on process and policy than passion and purpose. It can rely more on "the way we've always done things," forgetting that it was founded on "a better way to do things." Then, as times change and crises occur, the company realizes it has lost its capacity to be creative. The vision and energy of the founder has been lost. The company is in the process of losing its mission.[99]

Every now and again the church must refocus on the Founder's Mentality.

Someone has said, "An organization is dying when its memories are more vivid than its dreams."

Every now and again the church must refocus on the Founder's Mentality, on the Great Commission of our Founder, Jesus Christ.

> The Christians of today need some object great enough to engage all the powers of their minds and hearts. We find just such an object in the enterprise to make Christ known to the whole world. This would call out and utilize the best energies of the Church. It would help to save her from some of her gravest perils – ease, selfishness, luxury, materialism, and low ideals. It would necessitate, and therefore

greatly promote, real Christian unity, thus preventing an immense waste of force. It would react favorably on Christian countries. There is no one thing which would do so much to promote work on behalf of the cities and neglected country districts of the home lands as a vast enlargement of the foreign missionary operations. This is not a matter of theory; for history teaches impressively that the missionary epochs have been the times of greatest activity and spiritual vigor in the life of the home church. So the best spiritual interests of America, Great Britain, Germany, Australasia, and other Christian lands are inseparably bound up with the evangelization of the whole wide world. The dictates of patriotism, as well as of loyalty to our Lord, thus call upon us to give ourselves to the world's evangelization.[100]

Those words were written in the year 1900 by John R. Mott, the great American missionary strategist. They stirred a whole generation to the greatest mission enterprise since the first century! Thousands of young people joined the Student Volunteer Movement to take the message of Jesus to the world.

Fifty years later, God was once again moving the university students of the world – and a whole generation of sleeping, church-bound Christians – to refocus on the Great Commission.

Today I lay before you the greatest challenge ever given to man by the greatest person who has ever lived. No matter how wealthy, famous, brilliant, or powerful you may be, you will never give yourself to any cause that can compare with this life-changing, even world-changing, call of God. No matter how many honors, awards, or achievements may be placed in your hands, nothing can even begin to compare with this command of our Lord Jesus Christ to help take His message of love and forgiveness to every person in every community, in every city, in every country of the world and make disciples of all nations. Today we live in a world of rapid and radical change. Men's hearts are filled with fear and dread, frustration and despair. Mankind has proven incapable of coping with the pressing problems of our time: the population explosion, the pollution of the environment, the rising tide of crime and violence, sexual rebellion, alcoholism, drug addiction, abortion, pornography, urban sprawl, and wide spread political, social, and moral decay.

Oh, what an hour for Christians to become involved in the greatest spiritual harvest since Pentecost! This dark and desperate hour in the affairs of mankind is an hour of destiny, a time of unprecedented opportunity for Christians. This is the hour for which we were born: to set in motion a mighty, sweeping spiritual revolution that will turn the tide and reveal to mankind that the glorious gospel of our Lord Jesus Christ offers the basic solutions to every problem facing mankind."[101]

Thousands responded to Bill Bright's call and to the call of others, and as a result there are now two billion Christians in the world – more Christians in the year 2000 than there were *people* when John Mott wrote in 1900.

Now it is time to renew our efforts in the task of completing the Great Commission. It is God's heart, revealed in His Word from beginning to end.

There are more than ample reasons to give ourselves to the proclamation and demonstration of the good news of Jesus: He is the answer to every human, and He is the longing of every heart; everyone must have a chance to know Him for time and eternity.

There are reasons for hope that we can see the task completed in our generation.

There are reasons for hope that we can see the task completed in our generation: the development of global communications and new information technologies, the historic flourishing of church growth in the Global South, and the unprecedented and growing unity of the whole Body of Christ.

The mission is costly, but the reward is great.

On one occasion, Peter, reflecting on the course of his life, appealed to Jesus saying, *"We have left everything to follow you!"*

> *"Truly I tell you," Jesus replied, "no one who has left home or brothers or sisters or mother or father or children or fields for me and the gospel will fail to receive a hundred times as much in this present age: homes, brothers, sisters, mothers, children and fields – along*

with persecutions – and in the age to come
eternal life. But many who are first will be
last, and the last first" (Mark 10:28-31).

My wife and I considered this passage as we were making
our decision to leave a life of comfort in New England
and move to a former Soviet Muslim country for the
privilege of bringing the good news to a people who
had lived seventy years under atheistic communism
after a thousand years of Islamic domination. We were
excited to go, but like Peter, we were daunted by the cost.

I reflected on my own life to that point, in light of
Jesus' promise to give us one hundred times more than
we give up – in the present age. I was conceived as a
late-life mistake in an already failed marriage in a poor
town. My father was the proverbial neighborhood drunk
who swept up the bar for drinks and slept in the back
room after closing. My mom and I lived somewhere
below the poverty line for all of my growing-up years.

Then Jesus got hold of my life. Now I was sitting in
a comfortable house in a Boston suburb with a happy
marriage to a wonderful woman. I had five amazing
children, a loving church, four Harvard degrees, money
in my pocket, and the Red Sox in a pennant race!

Yet I was sensing God's call to give it all up – again.
Scriptures had been flooding into my mind for weeks
about seeing the unseen, about the heroes of the faith.
By faith Moses, when he had grown up, refused to be
known as the son of Pharaoh's daughter. He chose
to be mistreated along with the people of God rather
than to enjoy the fleeting pleasures of sin. He regarded

disgrace for the sake of Christ as of greater value than the treasures of Egypt, because he was looking ahead to his reward. By faith he left Egypt, not fearing the king's anger; he persevered because he saw him who is invisible (Hebrews 11:24-27).

Then this parable came to my mind: "The kingdom of God is like a riverboat gambler, who bets everything he has on one spin of wheel – and wins! And then pushes it all back out on the table for one more spin."

You won't find that one in the Bible, but God used it to help me understand what I was feeling. It was time for me to take my "hundred times as much" and put it back on the altar, in exchange for eternal

> It is time to "double down" on the Great Commission.

reward. Of course, there is really no gamble at all when we bet on Jesus; it just *feels* like one. (I could almost hear Kenny Rogers singing the altar call in the background: "You've got to know when to hold 'em, know when to fold 'em.")

Life is a series of decisions to give all that we are and everything we possess for the cause of making Him known. Every time we give it all up, He gives back a hundred times as much, until finally we die, and it all gets converted into eternal heavenly currency. Now that, my friends, is the true money laundering!

Jesus said, *Do not store up for yourselves treasures on earth, where moths and vermin destroy, and where thieves break in and steal. But store up for yourselves treasures in heaven, where moths and vermin do not destroy, and where thieves do not break in and steal.*

For where your treasure is, there your heart will be also (Matthew 6:19-21).

It is time to "double down" on the Great Commission, to clarify our vision, to become part of a concrete plan, to take action.

Dr. Bright used to close his talk on fulfilling the Great Commission by inviting those who heard him to pray a simple prayer. Let's pray that prayer together once again, as we renew our commitment to reach everyone, everywhere.

> *Dear Father in heaven, I stand at attention. I make myself available to You to do with as You wish. I surrender my life to the lordship of Jesus Christ totally, completely and irrevocably. I desire to be a man (woman) of God through whom You can bring Your message of love and forgiveness in Christ to all men everywhere. I invite You to cleanse me, to empower me, to lead me, to inspire me, to teach me, to enable me to do that which will bring the greatest honor and glory to Your name. Enable me by Your Holy Spirit to contribute my maximum time, talent and treasure to the fulfillment of the Great Commission in my time. I ask this in the wonderful name of the Lord Jesus. Amen.*[102]

Meet the Author

Erick Schenkel has served as Executive Director of the Jesus Film Project since 2012, bringing to this role a varied history of Christian service. After his graduation from Harvard College, Erick led a church-planting team that established a church and an elementary school in Arlington, Massachusetts. While leading this church, Erick earned two masters' degrees and a PhD from Harvard in the Study of Religion; his dissertation was published by Harvard University Press as *The Rich Man and the Kingdom: John D. Rockefeller, Jr., and the Protestant Establishment.* While in graduate school, Erick and his wife, Elizabeth, developed a desire to live and work in the Muslim world. The Schenkels moved to Muslim Central Asia in 1996, where Erick worked in the fields of education and economic development for eleven years. While in Central Asia, they also worked as church-planters alongside *JESUS* film teams, starting a Bible school and directing a movement of nationally led churches. Erick then served for five years as Strategy Director for North Africa, Middle East, and Central Asia for Campus Crusade for Christ. Erick became the third Executive Director of the Jesus Film Project in March 2012, succeeding Jim Green and founder Paul Eshleman.

The last photo taken before Erick and Elizabeth
were attacked in their home in Central Asia.

Erick's work in Central Asia involved providing
assistance to schools and universities.

Erick working with students in Central Asia.

Erick and Elizabeth today ministering
with the Jesus Film Project.

Jesus Film Project uses portable screens to take the Gospel to many corners of the earth, from deserts to forests and mountains to plains. Wherever there are people, Jesus Film Project aims to share the good news of Jesus Christ.

Now with ever evolving technology, Jesus Film
Project uses any mobile tool as a means of leveraging
the Gospel message into people's hands.

The Jesus Film App allows people all over the world to hear
the Gospel in their heart language. This tool is used by many
believers to share their faith in every corner of the earth.

The Jesus Film Project has had three Executive Directors: Jim Green, Paul Eshleman (founder) and Erick Schenkel.

Scan the QR code to watch the *JESUS* Film

Endnotes

Chapter One

1   "Statistics," Aboutmissions.org, accessed July 22, 2016, http://www.aboutmissions.org/statistics.html; "Statistics of World Missions," Hellwig Family, 2016, http://www.hellwig.com/en/statistics-of-world-missions/.

2   Paul Eshleman, *I Just Saw Jesus* (San Bernardino, CA: Here's Life Publishers, 1985).

3   Richard Foster, *Prayer: Finding the Heart's True Home* (New York: HarperCollins, 1992), 6

Chapter Two

4   Bill Bright, "Catch Excitement for the Gospel, Cru, https://www.cru.org/train-and-grow/transferable-concepts/help-fulfill-the-great-commission.html

5   Bright, "The What and Why of the Great Commission," Cru, https://www.cru.org/train-and-grow/transferable-concepts/help-fulfill-the-great-commission.3.html

Chapter Three

6   Ed Stetzer, "Preach the Gospel, and Since It's Necessary, Use Words," Christianity Today, June 25, 2012, http://www.christianitytoday.com/edstetzer/2012/june/preach-gospel-and-since-its-necessary-use-words.html; See also Jamie Arpin-Ricci, "Preach the Gospel at All Times?" The Huffington Post, July 1, 2012, http://www.huffingtonpost.com/jamie-arpinricci/preach-the-gospel-at-all-times-st-francis_b_1627781.html.

7   George M. Marsden, *Fundamentalism and American Culture*, (Oxford: Oxford University Press, 1985, 2006), 85; Richard Stearns, *The Hole in Our Gospel: What Does God Expect of Us* (Nashville: Thomas Nelson, 2010).

Chapter Four

8   William John, *History of the Marconi Company 1874-1965* (1972), 296.

9   "The Founding of Vatican Radio, February 12, 1931," http://www.vatican.va/news_services/radio/multimedia/storia_ing.html.

10   "History of Religious Broadcasting: 1920-1960: Background and Inferred Uses and Gratifications," myweb.arbor.edu/rwoods/.../LitRevHistoryReligiousBroadInferreduses.doc.

11   "The First Sixty Years," Trans World Radio, accessed July 21, 2016, https://www.twr.org/our-history.

12   David Harrell, "History in the Making – Pentecost at Prime Time," *Christian History*, Issue 49 (1996), https://www.christianhistoryinstitute.org/magazine/article/history-in-the-making-pentecost-at-prime-time/.

13   "About CBN," accessed July 21, 2016, http://www1.cbn.com/about.

14   "About Us," accessed July 21, 2016, http://www.tbn.org/about-us.

15   "SAT-7 History: Unbelievable!" accessed July 21, 2016, http://www.sat7.org/en/sat7/history.

16   Micha Kaufman, "The Internet Revolution is the New Industrial Revolution," *Forbes,* October 5, 2012, http://www.forbes.com/sites/michakaufman/2012/10/05/the-internet-revolution-is-the-new-industrial-revolution/#33ef6c8d5905.

17   Internet Live Stats, http://www.internetlivestats.com/internet-users/.

18   YouTube, http://youtube.com/yt/press/statistics.html.

19   "21 Completely Insane Social Media Statistics," *The Content Factory,* http://www.contentfac.com/more-people-own-cell-phone-than-toothbrush-10-crazy-social-media-statistics/.

20   Ericsson, June 3, 2015, accessed July 21, 2016, https://www.ericsson.com/news/1925907.

21   "JESUS" Film Project Story Archive (JFP Stories), April 2016.

22   JFP Stories, May 2014.

23   JFP Stories, April 2014.

24   JFP Stories, March 2016.

25   "Who Are Oral Learners," International Orality Network, https://orality.net/about/who-are-oral-learners/.

Chapter Five

26   Harvey Cox, *The Secular City: Secularization and Urbanization in Theological Perspective* (1965), Collier Books, 25th anniversary edition 1990; *Religion in the Secular City: Toward a Postmodern Theology,* (1985), Simon & Schuster.

27   "JESUS, HD Version," History video.

28   JFP Stories, June 2015.

29   JFP Stories, June 2016.

30   JFP Stories, July 2016.

31   JFP Stories, September 2014.

32   JFP Stories.

33   JFP Stories, June 2014.

34   JFP Stories, March 2016.

35   JFP Stories.

36   JFP Stories, March 2010.

37   JFP Stories, February 2012.

38   JFP Stories.

39   JFP Stories.

Chapter Six

40   Ecclesiastes 3:11b; Augustine, Confessions, 1.1; Blaise Pascal, *Pensées* VII (425).

41   JFP Stories, May 2015.

42   JFP stories, December 2013.

43   JFP Stories, February 2015.

44   JFP Stories, August 2013.

45   JFP Stories, May 2015.

46   Report to the author.

47   JFP Stories, January 2012.

48   JFP Stories, November 2013.

49   JFP Stories, January 2012, From *JESUS* Film Partnership of Global Partners (Wesleyan Church).

Chapter Seven

50   Donna Rachel Edmunds, "Claim: Every Five Minutes a Christian is Martyred for Their Faith," *Breitbart London*, 19 September 2015, http://www.breitbart.com/london/2015/09/19/claim-every-five-minutes-christian-martyred-faith/.

51   Open Doors, https://www.opendoorsusa.org/; Voice of the Martyrs, https://www.persecution.com/; International Christian Concern, http://www.persecution.org/.

52   JFP Stories, July 2012.

53   JFP Stories, March 2010, From The JESUS Film Partnership for Global Partners (Wesleyan church).

54   JFP Stories, November 2014.

55   JFP Stories, May 2010.

56   JFP Stories, June 2010.

Chapter Eight

57   "Christian Traditions," Pew Research Center, http://www.pewforum.org/2011/12/19/global-christianity-traditions/.

58   Much of the historical information in this section is from "Timeline

of Christians Missions," Wikipedia, July 4, 2016, accessed July 20, 2016. https://en.wikipedia.org/wiki/Timeline_of_Christian_missions#cite_note-barrettp24-21. Those who wish to go deeper may use the endnotes and citations in this wikipedia article to do so. See especially Mark & Ruth Dickens, "Church of the East Timeline," *Oxuscom.com*, 1999, accessed July 20, 2016; David Barrett, ed., *World Christian Encyclopedia*, Oxford University Press, 1982; Kenneth Scott Latourette, *A History of the Expansion of Christianity*, 7 volumes, (1938–45); Stephen Neill, *A History of Christian Missions*. Penguin Books, 1986; Gerald H. Anderson, ed., *Biographical Dictionary of Christian Missions*, Simon & Schuster Macmillan, 1998.

59   Global South definition from Wikipedia: https://en.wikipedia.org/wiki/Global_South.

60   call2all, "History of Table 71," March 9, 2012, YouTube. https://www.youtube.com/watch?v=hJ9D9g025CU.

61   "History and Impact," visionSynergy, *http://visionsynergy.net/history-and-impact/*.

62   Francis, *The Joy of the Gospel (Evangelii Gaudium)*, (United States Conference of Catholic Bishops, 2013). Sections 264.

63   Richard Lovelace, *Dynamics of Spiritual Life: An Evangelical Theology of Renewal* (Downers Grove: IVP Academic, 1979), 20-1.

Chapter Nine

64   Chris Sleath, "EKSWTFJ," unpublished research, 2013.

65   Philip Jenkins, *The Next Christendom: The Coming of Global Christianity* (Oxford: Oxford University Press, 2002); *The New Faces of Christianity: Believing the Bible in the Global South* (Oxford: Oxford University Press, 2008).

66   Jason Mandryk and Molly Wall, State of the World, YLG2016, August 2016, slide 5, https://www.lausanne.org/content/state-world-jason-mandryk-molly-wall-ylg2016. See also "Christianity in its Global Context, 1970-2020: Society, Religion and Mission," Center for the Study of Global Christianity, Gordon-Conwell Theological Seminary, June 2013, http://www.gordonconwell.edu/ockenga/research/documents/ChristianityinitsGlobalContext.pdf

67   Phillip Connor, "6 Facts about South Korea's Growing Christian Population," Pew Research Center, August 12, 2014, http://www.pewresearch.org/fact-tank/2014/08/12/6-facts-about-christianity-in-south-korea/; Samuel H. Moffett, "What Makes the Korean Church Grow," *Christianity Today*, January 31, 2007. (First published November 23, 1973).

68   William Blair and Bruce Hunt, *The Korean Pentecost and the Sufferings Which Followed* (Edinburgh: Banner of Truth Trust, 1977) in C. Hope Flinchbaugh, "A Century After North Korean Revival, Dreams of an Encore," *Christianity Today*, January 31, 2007, http://www.christianitytoday.com/ct/2007/januaryweb-only/105-32.0.html.

69   Flinchbaugh, 2-3. See also "Why South Korea is so Distinctively Christian," The Economist, August 12, 2014, http://www.economist. com/blogs/economist-explains/2014/08/economist-explains-6.

70   Sandra Park, "Rebuilding the "Jerusalem of the East: North Korea's Past, Present and Future," http://midwayreview.uchicago.edu/a/8/3/ park/park.pdf.

71   Katherine T. Phan, "Korean World Missions Conference Celebrates Milestone of 20,000 Korean Missionaries Worldwide," The Christian Post, July 27, 2012, http://www.christianpost.com/news/korean-world-mission-conference-celebrates-milestone-of-20000-korean-missionaries-worldwide-79015/.

72   Melissa Steffan, "The Surprising Countries Most Missionaries Are Sent From and To," Christianity Today, July 25, 2013, http://www. christianitytoday.com/gleanings/2013/july/missionaries-countries-sent-received-csgc-gordon-conwell.html.

73   See John McNeill, "Lessons from Korean Mission in the Former Soviet Region," International Bulletin of Missionary Research, Vol. 36, No 2, April 2012: 78-81.

74   Frances Martel, "Christianity Booming in Asia and Sub-Saharan Africa," Breitbart News Network, 19 December 2013, http://www. breitbart.com/national-security/2013/12/19/christianity-booming-in-asia-and-sub-saharan-africa/.

75   Maria Zandt, "The Situation of Christians in Sub-Saharan Africa," KAS International Reports, 33, Konrad Adenauer-Stiftung, 6/2011, http://www.kas.de/wf/doc/kas_23017-544-2-30.pdf?110606100737.

76   "The Global Religious Landscape," Pew Research Center's Religion & Public Life Project, 18 December 2012, accessed 14 February 2015.

77   "The Future of World Religions: Population Growth Projections, 2010-2050: Sub-Saharan Africa," Pew Research Center's Religion & Public Life Project, April 2, 2015, Accessed July 13, 2016, http:// www.pewforum.org/2015/04/02/sub-saharan-africa/.

78   "The Explosion of Christianity in Africa," Christianity.com, accessed July 13, 2016, http://www.christianity.com/church/churchhistory/ timeline/2001-now/the-explosion-of-christianity-in-africa-11630859. html.

79   Andrew Walls, "The Mission of the Church Today in the Light of Global History." Word and World XX, Number I, Winter 2000:17.

80   "[Life Story]—Bekele Shanko," YouTube, June 21, 2013, https:// www.youtube.com/watch?v=Nm-87GB_kZ0.

81   Global Alliance for Church Multiplication, https://gacx.io/.

82   Reported to author by ministry leader.

83   Jack Aldwinckle, "Why the Catholic Church Is Losing Latin America, and How It's Trying to Get It Back," Quartz, February 15, 2015. http://qz.com/342810/why-the-catholic-church-is-losing-latin-america-and-how-its-trying-to-get-it-back/.

84   Andrea Marcela Madambashi, "Half of Brazil's Population to be

Evangelical Christian by 2020," *The Christian Post,* February 20, 2011, http://www.christianpost.com/news/half-of-brazils-population-to-be-evangelical-christian-by-2020-49071.

85   Kenneth D. MacHarg, "Evangelical Christianity Thriving in Brazil," http://www.jesusforlife.net/Documents/Evangelical%20Christianity%20thriving%20in%20Brazil.pdf.

86   Xiaoling Zhu and Jimmy Carter, "Jimmy Carter and Bible Printing in China," *Global Ministries,* May 24, 2011, http://www.globalministries.org/news/eap/jimmy-carter-bible.html.

87   Emily Rauhala, "Christians in China Feel Full Force of Authorities' Repression," *The Washington Post,* December 23, 2015; "Christianity in China," *billionbibles.org, http://www.billionbibles.org/china/how-many-christians-in-china.html;* "Underground, Overground," *The Economist,* April 9, 2016.

88   Brother Yun, Peter Xu Yongze, Enoch Wang, and Paul Hattaway, *Back to Jerusalem: Three Chinese House Church Leaders Share Their Vision to Complete the Great Commission* (Downers Grove, IL: InterVarsity Press, 2003).

89   Michael Gryboski, "Trends in Christian Missions: Global Christianity Experts," *The Christian Post,* May 20, 2016, http://www.christianpost.com/news/5-trends-in-christian-missions-global-christianity-experts-164282/pageall.html.

90   "Christianity in its Global Context, 1970-2020."

91   Matt Ritsema, "Cambodia—Church Planting and Multiplication," YouTube, February 5, 2013, https://www.youtube.com/watch?v=7MrKR0GVw_s.

Chapter Ten

92   This is the vision statement of Campus Crusade for Christ, International—Cru, of which the Jesus Film Project is a part.

93   Cf. Eric Swanson, "Ministries and Movements," *Cru Press* 2010, https://www.cru.org/content/dam/cru/legacy/2012/03/Ministries-and-Movements.pdf.

94   Operation World, http://www.operationworld.org/join-prayer-movement; Joshua Project, https://joshuaproject.net/.

95   Charles Kiser, "David Watson and Church Planting Movements," *in the storyline.* https://inthestoryline.com/2009/05/18/david-watson-and-church-planting-movements/; David L. Watson, Website. http://www.davidlwatson.org/.

96   Alpha, http://alphausa.org/about/.

97   Steve Steele, "A Case Study in Cooperative Evangelism: The Dawn Model," for the Billy Graham Center Evangelism Roundtable "Toward Collaborative Evangelization," October 4-5, 2002, http://www.wheaton.edu/~/media/Files/Centers-and-Institutes/BGC/Roundtable/2002/2002-Steele.pdf.

98   GACX, https://gacx.io/.

Chapter Eleven

99   Bain and Company, "Founder's Mentality® and the paths to sustainable growth," *Bain and Company Insights.* https://www.youtube.com/watch?v=Rp4RCIfX66I.

100 John R. Mott, *The Evangelization of the World in This Generation (1900)*, 25.

101 Bill Bright, "Catch Excitement for the Gospel," Cru, https://www.cru.org/train-and-grow/transferable-concepts/help-fulfill-the-great-commission.1.html.

102 Bill Bright, "The Rewards and Costs of the Great Commission," Cru, https://www.cru.org/train-and-grow/transferable-concepts/help-fulfill-the-great-commission.1.html.

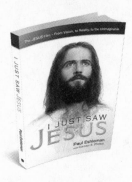

This miraculous story reveals how *JESUS* began as one man's vision and became a record-breaking film seen more than 9 billion times and convincing millions to follow Christ.

Volunteer film teams, missionaries, and pastors risk their lives daily, showing the film in remote tribes and villages, among religions that strictly prohibit Christianity, and even to the world's most elite and powerful leaders. They have overcome threats, witches' curses, and deadly diseases. The teams carry compact generators and portable projectors, often traveling by foot or horseback, bush plane or canoe. Their pure, unbridled joy comes from sharing *JESUS* with those who have not yet seen and heard the gospel.

Brian Deacon, the actor who portrays Jesus, speaks only words taken directly from the Gospel of Luke. As biblically accurate as possible, the *JESUS* film is taking Jesus to the world's men, women, and children in their own heart language. Translated into more than 1,400 languages, with more planned, this film is changing the world. *JESUS* is being seen and heard, and His words are proving as powerful today as they were 2,000 years ago.

Available at JesusFilmStore.com.